Dark Songs

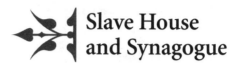 Slave House
and Synagogue

Books by Laurence Lieberman

Poetry

Dark Songs: Slave House and Synagogue   (1996)

The St. Kitts Monkey Feuds   (1995)

New and Selected Poems: 1962–92   (1993)

The Creole Mephistopheles   (1989)

The Mural of Wakeful Sleep   (1985)

Eros at the World Kite Pageant   (1983)

God's Measurements   (1980)

The Osprey Suicides   (1973)

The Unblinding   (1968)

Criticism

Beyond the Muse of Memory:
Essays on Contemporary American Poets   (1995)

Unassigned Frequencies:
American Poetry in Review   (1977)

The Achievement of James Dickey   (1968)

Dark Songs

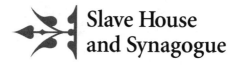 Slave House
and Synagogue

POEMS BY
Laurence Lieberman

THE UNIVERSITY OF ARKANSAS PRESS
Fayetteville   *1996*

00   99   98   97   98   5   4   3   2   1

Designed by Gail Carter

⊖ The paper used in this publication meets the minimum
requirements of the American National Standard for Permanence
of Paper for Printed Library Materials   Z39.48-1984.

Library of Congress Cataloging-in-Publication Data

Lieberman, Laurence.
     Dark songs : slave house and synagogue : poems / by Laurence Lieberman.
          p.   cm.
     ISBN 1-55728-409-1 (cloth : alk. paper). — ISBN 1-55728-410-5 (pbk. : alk. paper)
     1. Caribbean Area—Poetry.   I. Title
PS3562.I43D37   1996
811'.54—dc20   95-49128
                                              CIP

for Mariah Danielle and Dylan Laurence

Acknowledgments

I wish to thank the editors of the following magazines, in which these poems first appeared: *American Poetry Review:* "Epidermal Hell," "Smuggled Pencil Stubs," "Cudjoe's Head"; *The Caribbean Writer:* "Freedom Spurned"; *The Chariton Review:* "Names Scrawled on the Priests' Satin Robes"; *The Cimarron Review:* "Life Shock"; *Denver Quarterly:* "In Fear of the Music Scholar"; *The Gettysburg Review:* "Wharf Angel"; *The Hudson Review:* "I.V. Runaway," "White Tiger and the Mosquitoes"; *The Kenyon Review:* "Lifestyles Prince"; *The Nation:* "Saviour of Assassins," "House Walk over the Mountain"; *New England Review:* "Carib's Leap," "The Ballad of Garfield John"; *Partisan Review:* "Sleuths"; *Pequod:* "Dark Songs: Slave House and Synagogue"; *Sewanee Review:* "The St. Kitts Monkey Feuds" parts 1 and 2 (excerpt); and *The Southern Review:* "Shirma: Witness from Carriacou," "Brangwen: Witness from Frankfurt."

"Dark Songs: Slave House and Synagogue" was reprinted in *The Best American Poetry 1991,* edited by Mark Strand.

"The St. Kitts Monkey Feuds" was published in a limited edition of 200 copies by Harry Duncan at The Cummington Press.

Special thanks to the Center for Advanced Study at the University of Illinois for a creative writing fellowship, which supported the completion of this book.

Contents

 I

Dark Songs

St. Eustatius

Dark Songs: Slave House and Synagogue

(St. Eustatius, Summer 1989)

1.

A few museum florid paintings by unknown
colorists, but mostly sketches
    in private family albums tell the story—
we children more inclined to trust
    tales we heard of slave days on Granddad's knee
at bedtime than the remote sagas
    we find in our school books today . . . A shipment
of new slaves came, all at once,
    several boatfuls clumped in a caravan:

serfs in one lead vessel, an echelon or two
above their comrades in chains
    in rear ships, parallel teams of rowers
puffing at the oars to speed
    those sail-masted, multi-sail-driven craft.
The privileged half-freed advance
    troop, whether promoted by bribes, loyalties,
friendship, sexual favors,
    family rank honored across generations,

or sheer beauty and power of person—those few,
alone, were earmarked for serf
    status: no, not branded or pegged like livestock,
but targeted for low-rank jobs.
    Perhaps no more than four hundred per installment
(from Ghana, Rhodesia), leg-cuffed,
    they were herded like steer—while that vanguard
of cooks, domestics, saddle-
    horsers, disembarking first, arranged floor mats

to sleep the maximum number per human stall
in the deep low-ceilinged bins
　　of the two-story slave quarters. Chefs, tailors,
laundresses, who slept in makeshift
　　huts or tents in the rearyard, had, at least,
some leg room, *private bodyturn space.*
　　In the slavehouse, itself, all girls and ladies
were ensconced upstairs, while men
　　and boys were marooned to the ground floor.

　　　　2.

　　　　When both levels
　　　　　grow full to capacity, most slaves
　　　are sandwiched in boxy
　　　　　tight jamups—vertical by day,
　　　horizontal
　　　·by night: except for sharp jabs in belly, neck, eyes
　　　　　or tendrest parts (breasts, genitals),
　you often don't know your neighbor's knees, elbows,
　bony appurtenances
　　　(keen-edged, wiry, if underfed on sea
　　　voyage, as like as not)
from your holy own;

　　　　but your howls
　　　　　and smart pains—excruciating, most,
　　of whip's lash—define you,
　　　　no confusing your boneaches,
　　muscle spasms,
　　nausea, or skin rash rawness with your floormate's
　　　scorched hide: when skin and bone's

so mashed, mine into the others, I into Thou,
agonies keep self
    intact; tiniest remove between Spirit
    entity and entity saves.
Who we be survives. . . .

        Some weak slaves,
            afflicted with permanent squared
        shoulder, humped back,
            limbs flattened and malformed,
        were disabled
        by the crunch of bodies; no few lads suffocated
            between more muscular hall mates,
    none to blame. At intervals, when slavehouse
    quotas ran amok,
            open market ships, from South America
            and other more distant ports,
arrived: bids for slaves

            at townsquare
            auction commenced by first light; each
        half dozen, or thereabouts,
                placed on front doorstoop auction
        block, in cluster;
        some bidders coerced by shrewd auctioneer to purchase
            a mixed gaggle of males, females,
    young and old, as one indivisible unit—to speed up
    haggling over prices,
            finicky tooth checks, sight and hearing tests,
            as if man needed model-perfect
molars, 20/20 sight,

just to chop
and husk cane all day in the fields;
or lass glamour-shaped hips
and breasts just to scoop proper
bounteous handfuls
of cotton. Each flock might boast a matchless beauty,
or prize strongarm—most slaves sold
for export to distant shores, Statia being chief
transshipment center
for humans, and non-human goods, alike,
throughout the Antilles chain
of isles. . . . Before selloffs

in human meat
markets, a normal day in the yards
finds cooks, like modern
caterers, stacking huge supplies
of fast-food grub,
laundresses hauling wagons and carts with mountains
of soiled sackcloth pullovers, baggy
shapeless blouse and shorts, all alike in style,
dull yellowish gray,
loose crosshatched weave of material;
a few sizes are to be stretched
to cover widest spectrum

of body shapes,
women and men in identical garb,
little telling them apart. . . .
I peer into the two-story-deep
structure, thin bricks
marvelously even-mortared, still intact today

but for the very few crumbled
or missing slim yellow units; those narrow
interior hallways
    resemble storage bins or blank vats
    in grain elevators, hardly
fit stable for livestock,

        much less brain-
        bearing-mammal biped repository;
    so few narrow windows, shrunk
        to prevent runaways, perhaps,
    are raised too high
    to collect inflow of trade winds, no East-West matchup
        for air streams or ripples of cross-
ventilation: if the inmates weren't asphyxiated
by closest body
    cramping, that crush of backs and hips,
    they might choke on stale fetors,
so noxious was the stench. . . .

    3.

Josser Daniel, my tutor, points across the road,
shoreside, directly opposite
Ye Old Slave House: yet another shipman's stock
quarters fallen into disuse,
    idle for one hundred years or more, boarded up.
This was "de Guvment Guardhouse
    and Constabulary joined" (court, too, I suppose,
all functions of arrest, trial,
    and jail terms centralized for speedy work shifts) . . .

When British Rear Admiral Rodney laid siege
to Statia, he plundered the gold-
     and-silver vaults. Statia, dubbed *Golden Rock*,
had been the wealth jugular—
     sea trade megalopolis of the whole Eastern
Caribbean—for decades.
     Like today's duty-free Colonies, espoused
for their money-laundering
     schemes via offshore banks, Statia was haven

     for tax evaders at home, drawn to price steals
on ritziest goods the Continent
     shipped abroad, at bargain basement markoffs.
Quick as Rodney shut down the Port
     with his naval blockade, he set about to fleece
all wealthy merchants—then tried
     to win sympathizers among the local poorfolks.
But a few outspoken mavericks
     painted him History's worst *blackguard, pirate,*

     barbarian, quoting wild Biblical parallels
in both Old and New Testaments
     (so oral historians tell), packed to deliver
the most stinging word portraits
     of his "atrocities" you can imagine, the sole
weapon any might wield against him.
     Sir Rod held all the guns. But ah, what threats
they mustered! The few unnamed—
     though prestigious—writers in their midst

     would spread poison about him to a World Press
(such Global media exchange as
     was viable 200 years back): they'd brand him

close kin to Attila the Hun!
 Since his most acid and eloquent accuser
was a prominent Jew, Rod staged
 a surprise police raid on a Friday night
Shabbas Service—in full swing
 in the Upper Town Oranjusted synagogue.

 Hah! Sham holy service, a covert political
town meeting, in disguise, Jews
 plotting sabotage against occupation forces,
so Rodney would bluster and plead
 in his own defense, years later in High Court,
when he answered to charges sworn
 upon him into the docket by Queen's Counselor:
ACTS OF MASS ANTI-SEMITISM
 AND RELIGIOUS CALUMNY disgracing the Crown.

4.

 Rodney's armed guards,
 undetected, surround the old Synagogue
 where all but a smidgin of some three-hundred-odd
 adult Statian Jews
 are congregated, arrest them en masse
(not a soul among them can slip
 through Rodney's net), and swiftly transport the lot
 to this Guardhouse, three ships at the ready, armed to gunnels'
 galley teeth, all sails furled to deport them—
 the whole Congregation:
 chainlocked indoors, thrashing and howling, for fear
 they be pilloried, throttled, lynched, or rent
 by firing squads

          at daybreak. . . . Before dawn,
    they're whisked to the pier, ropetied in threes
       or foursomes, mouths gagged, heads bag-covered
             to cloak their faces
       from stray passersby (though all citizens
are warned by Curfew Broadsides
          to stay indoors or risk police detainment,
         not to say sniper fire); those who resist, the hysterics,
   flinging themselves sideways or backwards on the wharf,
          are dragged aboard
             by their heels, heads clumping like loose potatoes
       in the sacks; those upright, the stoics,
             are stampeded

          from dock to shipdeck—
    the whole forced exodus carried off, lickety
          split, in ten minutes flat. . . . Thus, the near bulk
             of Island Jewry,
       third and fourth generation Dutch families
who hail back to the civic
          roots of Colonial days, are Shanghaied, lugged
       to twelve-miles-distant St. Kitts, abandoned on woodsy
shoreline: huge death bounties sworn on their heads,
       if their postered mugs
          be spotted in Statia. . . . Sir Rodney's return home,
       months hence, greeted by scathing headlines
             in London Press:

          ATTACKS ON DUTCH JEWS
       DEPLORED BY HOLLAND, Admiral Rodney's conduct
          in Statia viewed as "heinous, verging on Holy War,
          and UN-BE-COM-ING

to any agent of Her Majesty the Queen
on the High Seas," these charges
        upon Rodney's honor carrying far more sting
        than vandalism, pillaging or no-holds-barred piracy
    (the latter, just the spoils of war by a turn
        of the tongue); no record's
            extant that Rodney had slain even one Jew—
    but his impulse to wipe the whole Isle's
            Jew-smudged slate

        clean, at a single stroke,
    smacks of the Third Reich's mass roundups. Secret
        abduction of Jews in trucks, railways boxcars, army
            transports to the camps;
        their sly, devious ruses to keep pervasive
body-snatching under wraps
        for those many months. . . . Why, despite Rod's
        early departure, did so few Jewish deportees ever return
    to Statia? Perhaps the small nation's strand
        bore his taint in offshore
            mists, a noxious fume of ill spirit hung
        suspended in the ghostly sea air . . .
            Today, I explore

        the awesome blank ruins
    of Synagogue where the worshipers were entrapped,
        a grand void since their going, perhaps never once
            immersed in formal prayer
        after that day; these walls may never again
have been graced with Cantor's
            voice waves, or pupil's mime-whispered breath
        chants of Old Testament prayer, some murmured orthodoxy

of those displaced Jerusalemites smitten
from this sad haven
ever afterwards . . . And do I hear, again, the song
of davening, Cantor's sweet lullaby
of trilled scripture,

the youngest children,
students of Hebrew reading from the back
of the holy book toward the front, their fingers
groping as they trace
those richly rounded letters of Hebrew script
alphabets from right to left
while they repeat, soundlessly, with their lips
the Cantor's operatic blessings . . . *Driven, blindfolded*
and gagged, bag-shroud-faceless from homeland,
a family of spirits,
dug up by their roots, torn from the soil & hurled
across the sea, from one tiny Carib
outpost to the next.

 II

Carib's Leap
Grenada

Carib's Leap

Heyling Charles, alias Pali Wali, recounts how his mother died
      last year, this very week,
  at age seventy-six; mine two years back, to the day,
    just six weeks shy of her eightieth birth
month—*too soon, too too young,* we sigh in vocal duet: together,
     five beers downed
  apiece, we stand on the cliff-ledge overlook
    at CARIB'S LEAP, and mourn
      the demise
   of mothers. . . . I shake off
the municipal sea mists, while we survey
  a diversity
of stones in this small graveyard—flanking the Sauteurs public
   grade school: a few larger slabs, markers
crowning the plots of turn-of-the-Century prominent
    citizens, seem half-dislodged
from their moorings in loose untended sod. One tall rectangle,

         engraved with gold script, nods,
           as if top heavy,
     from the cliff skull's receding hairline: grave
          of the town's one-time
Minister of Finance. Now we make
     a half-hearted attempt, Heyling Charles and I,

to prop up the loose fake-marbly column, incised with tributes
    of ornate Romanesque scrawl
lauding the one civil servant who always balanced
   de town's shaky budget, keeping de blue
collar worker citizenry's payroll checks solvent, and town monies
   in de black.

We pile up mossy rocks around the tombstone
    and brush loose dirt and gravel
        in earthen
    cracks to steady the mount.
    We take turns. One shoulders the Pisa-angled
        tablet upright,
    while the other stuffs firm landfill in gaps under the base. . . .
    Our moms, too, were shrewd and frugal
money jugglers—we the legatees of such thrift:
        both *only* sons, both orphaned
in middle age, but no less devastated by that parental void

            than if we'd been teenagers.
                O we are half
        teens, still, half Mid-Century lads! And today,
                boy half swallows man,
    as we tipsy two, asway, invoke a Spirit
            of our mothers—both snatched from us by *Strokes.* . . .

And here stood they, all arms twined in a last communal embrace,
        some forty-odd survivors
    of the Carib tribe, men, women, small babes & toddlers
        in whatever proportion (no one knows
    the exact number), their Spaniard pursuers clamoring at their backs.
        Whatever Fate
        beckoned—slaughter by musket fire, burnings
            at the stake, or most dreaded
                enslavement
            to those fish-belly-faced
    Conquistadores—they chose, all of One Voice Howl
            in the trade winds,

same winds as today, to die   and yes, *die out*   in one Mystic
            synchronized bold LEAP of defiance
to the naked rocks below. They knew their family
            multitude of spirits, the clan
Over-Soul, would *fly up,* while their hand-clasped lean bodies gored

                on the horned rock pinnacles
                    below, and soar
            into a life beyond, a life forevermore remote
                    from *terrible nonsense,*
        terrible nonsense (Pali Wali's words,
                himself an unbookish man) *of dem White Barbarians. . . .*

Gull screech. Two frigatebirds lunge for the feathered small game
            overhead—the prolonged shrieks
    may be Caribs adrift on the wind updrafts, or perhaps
        they may be our two mothers, in chorus,
    quavering   *it's allright   we, too, are at peace   spared life's*
            last terrible
        nonsense   here we are   O we do continue
            just as you last remember
                us   only sons
            our beauty intact   you know
        how it grew ever stronger in Age   peaked. . . .
            My mom, but two days
    before she died, had her hair done up spiffy by her favorite
            beautician. We sat in the Cuban-Chinese
    family diner awaiting our entree. The chef's twelve-
            year-old petite daughter,
who served us, kept staring and staring at Anita, always finding

more pretext to come back, ever
back, to our table.
Water refills. Extra Fortune Cookie (my first
fortune strip drew
a blank) . . . At last, she could contain
herself no more, and blurted out: *Senora, you are*

so beautiful, your hair, so beautiful, I've never seen anyone look so,
so, so . . . Mother looked puzzled
and mildly annoyed. *O what can she possibly mean*
by that? she asked the mute tablecloth.
But who *could* explain? I merely repeated the child's plain words,
they were true,
and from me, her only son, she would accept—
if vaguely—their drift. . . .
Drab schoolhouse
to one side, Catholic Church
across the path, the horror and violence
of Old Grenada's
darkest day seem effaced, dulled, by the bland civic exteriors.
And below, the many thick shrubs and sea-
resistant low trees seem to shroud those jagged rocks,
to blunt all rugged pointy spires
that burst open soft bellies, ribcages and thighs of the self-flung

families, crushed limbs or skulls
like so many soft-
rinded melons hurled at the sharp cutting edges. We
may suppose they aimed
themselves—like practiced Sky Divers
or parachutists—at the most keen-rimmed silhouettes

flashing below, honed by the sea's whetstone to a razor's hairline
      cutting edge, their bodies looping
   in glory of their last aerial dance, last dream flight.
     And yes, we do see them steering their plunge
  to greet, headforemost, the punishing raw angles of rock, welcoming
      that Great Howl
    of speediest death, the surest brain-crushers
     most dear, O yes, most fiercely
      sought after. . . .

Shirma: Witness from Carriacou

1.

Lunch with Shirma
at pierside restaurant on stilts:
tossing her bangs—that dreamy panache
which is her wont—she proposes we two ferret out
some grand, if elusive, locales,
a bit off the tourist beaten path. . . . At next table,
three engineers (on weekend
holiday from work at the new chemical
plant in Barbados)
insist I visit *pronto* the hilltop
bombed-out ruins,
jaggedly silhouetted on the skyline
across St. George's Bay.
I can feel Shirma cringe, though her face conceals
her anguish—*O that's the last place*
she'd happily go. When the factory trio drives off,
she asks me, pouty-lipped, why I'd wish
to see a mere "moshed shambles
of crumbled brick."

Before I can reply, she springs
to her feet—sputters, "Let's split. I'll take you."
In fifteen minutes winding ascent, we reach the summit
barrens: three to four years
since the invasion, and sadly, no one
has yet commenced to remove, or repair, the war-torn gutted
historic posh hotel
converted to Cuban militia headquarters.

A few bombed-out
            segments flattened to the ground,
                deep craters, symmetrical circles in place
        of one-time basement and foundations; other segments
                untouched, left standing, shakily,
            to a great four-story height, imminent safety hazard
        both to the vast turnover
    of eyewitness visitors and to hillside
        homes nestled below,
perched in the drop-off high-risk zone—debris
        poised to hit roofs
    or gables, as from a bombardier's well-aimed
        bombsight, the war casualties
            likely to resume if vandals or big storm winds upset
                the delicate balance of oblongs,
            teetery wall monoliths: a few standing on end, huge
                upright dominoes, most others cracked
                and leaning awry, but unbudged
                    for now . . . Shirma,

    choking back tears, tries to outline
        the background of this queer shattered monument—
            breaks down, comes clean with the story of her own chance
                entrapment in the freakish
                    war launched by our invasion forces'
        surprise attack. She, an *illegal alien* from small neighboring
                islet Carriacou (one
            of Grenada's petit Grenadines: homeland

of "the gentlest souls,
              Larry, the most peaceful citizens
              you could ever hope to meet"), ferries over,
          twice yearly, to Grenada for peaks of the tourist season,
              since jobs are scarce abroad. Shy lady
          of reddish-orange-tipped brown high-piled hair, twenty-five
      and quiet sexy, those slow hip
  swings as she ambles, much evident come-on
      to men half-tempered
by modest droop of lashes, charming pout
      before she speaks,
  whether tired, a bit ill, or mildly phlegmatic
      and passive in the way she retards
          her carriage behind her forward arms' thrust as she leans
              at bridge railing, shrewdly catching eyes
          of all passing motorists—*myself the day we first met.*
              "Look at this rattletrap wreck, once noble
              high-class guest house" (now literal
                  rat heap, I see,

  several large rodents scurrying
      in neglected trash piles): "Squashed like a roach!
          Brute excess of firepower horridly dumped on this harbor
              town, population center
                  crammed with kids, moms, goats, and mules—
      so few soldiers! Why smash up our homes, markets, with volleys
              of mortar shells falling
          like ugly hail all about us, noplace to hide?"

2.

You, a writer,
the soft life of privilege, work
is play and travel: you can't imagine
what it was like for me to find myself stunned, hanging laundry
in my yard in midtown, three streets
from the pier. When the first charge of rockets popped off,
I took puzzled sidelong glances,
absently went on with my hangers, clothespins,
neatly filling the line
with my duds. I supposed vulgar fireworks
were fast exploding
for a holiday celebration unbeknownst to me,
since I skip local news, often,
for days or weeks at a time; but after the first pause
of some minutes, I heard shells
discharge nearby, much louder than before. I swung round
to face this very hill across the bay
at the terrible moment. Oh, Lord!
Two helicopters

dropped their ugly payload on both roofs
of this fortress: tall flames and smoke poured forth
like a huge volcano blowing its top. And I'll never forget
I saw three uniformed
tiny stick figures spinning like cartwheels,
flying higher than the puzzle-piece chunks of roof which sprayed
in all directions, big hunks
of confetti, but no party favors or parade

baubles, these . . .
    I knew terror and dread at once,
        but I still didn't translate my glimpse
  of those toy stick-dolls into humans until the third blast,
      fierce shells clamoring right in my ears,
    some smoke puffs and fireballs bursting so close to my face
    I could feel the heat of them
on my temples a half second later. And I could
    nearly reach out my arm
to touch flames in the window curtains of a house
    next door; and then,
the shock that sent me running for cover (Don't ask
    why I didn't try to hide sooner;
      numb disbelief, I guess): I saw body parts, two limbs,
      a severed head, shooting upwards, mixed
      randomly with lamps, ceiling fixtures, wallpaper, and roof
        shingles in the house two doors away.
    Who could forget that bald head
      zooming like cannon-

ball skyward, then swallowed in smoke gush?
    I tried to look away, *tried*, but my gaze was stuck
      in strange excitement and rush of heart thumps too much
        like joy or good sex
          to believe, now, as I recall the exact
sensations, four years back—so grotesquely stark in mind's eye,
      it could be five minutes ago
    or one long moment, neverending, in dreams

or nightmares I
keep rehashing. . . . As I say, I ran
and hid under the bed before I fancied
hunting for cover, my afterimage of dismembered body parts
so intense, I wasn't sure if I'd left
the scene of carnage yet, my head buried under three pillows,
my ass and shoulders jammed
beneath the bedsprings, fists in my ears: I pushed
with all my God-given
might to block the neighbors' screams of agony
from my eardrums'
unstoppable chomps at all the worst sounds going,
as if each of my hungry ears
was a cannibal mouth devouring flesh of my torn kinfellows,
no silencing those teeth in my ears
rat-a-tat-tat chattering away through my thin hand shields.
For days, then, abiding the cruelest
soundless quiets I've even known,
I didn't stir

a finger, couldn't bring myself to budge
from the cave hollow under box springs and mattress,
not even to slink to the washroom: I had to keep shifting
my floor roosts to avoid
fresh puddles of tinkle, or drenched rug
patches grown rank, fetid; nor could I retrieve a single piece
of my linens from the line—
oddly, none was soiled in the four days' war.

Brangwen: Witness from Frankfurt

Kitchen staff
    two hours late for breakfast,
      I surmise I'm the solo overnight guest
in seaview midtown hotel (priced
too low, travel agents won't hear of it); but Brangwen
        appears, a morning rose
bow-tied to her hair: sixtyish, alert, seasoned
global traveler
          on holiday from Frankfurt.
For six years, without lapse,
she's frequented this quiet Inn for months in late winter

or early spring,
    both loveliest times of year,
      safely between two main tourist gluts.
We take our tea and biscuits,
served by last night's security guard, who moonlights
        at bar and snack counter—
in lieu of late first waitress. . . . We must feel past
hurdle of accents.
          Speech comes slow, but gains
savor, piquancy,
as we find simpatico, become fast friends, the divergence

of heritage
    and homeland a spur, tonic
      to vigor of conversation; soon, my Frau
drifts back three years to images
of St. George's Harbor, a traffic-gorged Carenage
        and long Grand Anse Beach
just one month after the invasion by militias
of six Carib lands

                    spearheaded by U.S. Marine
"task force": *Dead center
hit. Bull's Eye!* She can see my appetite is hotly piqued,

my cheek eager
        for the lash: anti-Reagan
        thrashing that I assume—too prone for Yankee
putdown—will be forthcoming. . . .
Her first walk down the pier, two teams of helicopters
        came cruising overhead
at intervals of a quarter-hour, flying so low
as they spun out
            above rooftops across the street,
she saw prop blades flash
in the sun, blindingly, before she heard the motors approach,

ducked—pure instinct!—
        as if dark bombs might fall.
        Did they strike terror in your heart? I ask.
*Oh no! Just surprise, they caught me
off guard, but a welcome sight,* she replies. *And did you
            approve the military
occupation?* She laughs: *Oh, the American troops,
they'd soon enough leave.*
                Those first weeks after the rout
of Cubans, Russians, Libyan
mercenaries, they kept a vigil, daily search for rumored

snipers, escapees,
        renegades loose in the hills;
        circling and circling, they nailed fugitive
quarry, two or three times a day,
at first: deported the aliens back to Cuba, the Mid-East.

It's true, armored trucks
were encamped on the beach, but posed no threat
to citizens, or guests
            like herself (*unless you be frisked
packing a revolver,
as were teenage hooligans), and she felt safe from muggers.

No *true* fascist
      takeover, the people welcomed it,
      rejoiced in a rescue from Bishop's assassins,
thugs. When Russians or Cubans
move into a place, they don't ever mean to leave. *Slave
            States. Afghanistan. Hungary.*
She'd been furious with her West German Premier's
attacks on Reagan, felt
            dismayed by *Soft-on-Cuba Factions*
in local St. George's
Press, but the U.S. Press fumbled far worse in undermining

the happy result,
      here . . . Politically obtuse,
      she finds me; she'll pictorialize her vision.
Scenes unfold: Russian planes
dropping supposed gifts for children—labeled CARE
            packages—over Afghanistan.
Untutored kids in the hills and rural districts
unwrap the pencil
            bombs: their eyes gouged out, limbs
shredded off at elbow
or shoulder like stalks of celery snapped. Exposed vessels,

tubes, dangled
      from sockets. She's seen live

films of the victims, herself, in pirated
underground home movies—smuggled
indoors. Or she'd have me compare the plight of Russia's
    seventeen million slaves
in East Germany—vast numbers of homeless waifs,
no jobs, impoverished,
       with thriving West Germany's
sixty-five million.
Why, do I suppose, so many, even today, risk their lives

to gundown by armed
    sentries—scaling the Berlin Wall
    and racing across the border? Or consider
the French, worse yet, in their all-out
merciless slaughter of Algerians. Or island street crime.
    After seven years' visits
to Port-of-Spain, Trinidad, she'll never go back,
she and three best friends
      brutally mugged in Queen's Park. Midday
crowds. No one helped. Royal
Mounted Police shrugged off their story of the beatings! . . .

What's your Faith?
    she asks. After a pause, *Jewish,*
    I—snappishly—reply, wondering, what's next?
I stare the God and Church question
back at her. Unasked, she rejoins: *My one and only God,*
    no Churchgoer, is to help
other folks poorer than myself. As for Faith,
Belief, I have enough
    and then some, for I can breathe
life force back into friends
who have lost hope, will to live, like a lifeguard reviving

half-drowned swimmers
    with mouth-to-mouth. Heart massage.
        When her husband was released from *The Camps*,
no doctor or local hospitals
could do anything for him, he'd lost eighty pounds, forgot
        how to care for himself,
or *to care*. She vowed, she'd nurse him, impossibly,
back to health. Four years,
        it took, of steadfast heart & spirit
I.V. transfusions.
But today, she swears he's whole, he's every tad the man he was

before *The Camps*.
    She kept telling him she'd bring
    him back from the dead, like coaxing a stubborn
donkey, and she did. *Where is he*
now? I ask. He can't travel with her this year. He works
        for the Frankfurt Road Service,
manages teams of derelict roadsweep crews, keeps
them in line, roads & paths
        must be disencumbered of snow
in Europe's worst winter
for decades. *Begs Brangwen to come home trailing an empty purse.*

Sleuths

At the gate to The Inner Bar, a tap on my shoulder (more
a prod)—I spin about,
      while Samson blurts: *you, Mafia man!* . . .
I stand accused,
veer left, can't get my tongue unstuck. *No, no way,*
      I stammer. My reply
gets his goat, very pissed, I've robbed or cheated him:
Better you learn to use de English
      language krecktly, America, Monsieur,
      stomps away. Next man, coming up
the spiral stairs,

         kindly eyes, tells me: *Samson is chief Don, hereabouts.*
           Mafioso druglord
        of de whole neighborhood. I should never
           be out, solo,
        on the streets past 9. *You hab de wrong skin color*
          on your face. I charge
      downstairs to The Inner Bar, an open courtyard between
        three apartments. Rooms, facing the yard,
      do double duty as front parlor and public
      alehouse, wherein Farouk and rock-
           star brother

Dagoo, beckoning, invite me to join them for down-home
snacks, who lustily slurp
      spinachy callaloo soup, boiled
chicken & yams.
Tipped off by insiders, I'm a journalist for *Time,*
      Newsweek, or some Bigtime
U.S. Papers, they offer me lunch, to be accompanied

by boombox hit tunes and the free scoop
        on Grenada politics, all the War Sagas—
    no thanks to eats, say I, but yes
to talespinning,

                for who can resist the stories? Farouk unveils lowdown
                                on the local druglord
                    wars: U.S. Marines, don't I know,
                                    first introduced
                hard drugs to Grenada; Yankee veteran dope pushers
                        set up the networks—
            thriving business ever since. Kingpins kill one another
                        off, every few months, in battle
                for the best turfs. And when they get itchy
                    jousting for power, *we lay low,*
                            hoping to stay

out of crossfires. Jus' dis week, duh heat's on. So tings
be comin' to a boil!
        Doors fly open. I stop writing,
fold my notepad.
Ex-minister of Finance Gascoyne fumes alcohol
            and spitfire cusswords,
bull-ruttish in fury, for I'd spurned his thick-tongued
slurpy rambles, hours back. No mercy.
        No forgiving my insult. He points a shaky
        finger down at me, seated there:
it is I, none

        other, who be the accursed nemesis he'd warned them about.
                            Better hold your tongues,
            says he, crab-pincering his thumb

                              and forefinger
              tongs at each would-be informer mouth, much as if
                         he'd twist and yank out
        any moist member leaking State Secrets to one such as me:
                   a dangerous spy, he'd have them know,
              I'll sell their stories for big bucks (no fee,
                    no concessions for them) to smut
                              mags of Hollywood.

Or worse, I may stick them in my own books; he's read them
all, packs of lies, no truth
             in any page. . . A new tack, I work
for police spy
enclave, so I'll bring CIA lawmen down on their necks. . . .
             No one pays him mind,
but it's a challenge to hear each other over his ravings.
My notepad back in action now, info
             moving fast between us, while Right Honorable
             Gascoyne's switched from Security
Guard to sleuth mode,

             he stands close to my neck, peeps over my shoulder & scans
                              the jottings with blasé
              I-told-you-so smirks. Soon he mumbles
                              under his breath
              few words he can make out, as if defusing the charge
                    of my wild script and scrawl
        by working the tart gumballs of syllables round and round
                    in his pouchy cheeks; he spits, from time
              to time, expunging plugs of foul noun-and-verb
                    tobacco! So I withdraw my little
                              journal pad, snap

it shut. *Ah, YOU are the spy,* I say. *Indeed not,* says he. *I
am INTELLIGENCE.* Silence . . .
           Two barmen, wheeling their portable
jiffy hooch carts
about the courtyard, traipse into our soup kitchen
          armed with raggedy dogeared
yellow manuscripts. Both have *major exposés* in progress,
says one—*his* only drawback, he lacks
       the finesse and niceties of my Highbrow
       Education; chirps the other,
his book's all set

         to go to Press, but he'll be needing my few moments *assist
                   with grammar and sentence
            hookups. . .* And as I edge backwards
                 through the gate, Ex-
Minister Gascoyne scolds, whenever I do publish
       my most *dastardly writings*
about their lives, I had better refrain from terming
         their fair parlorscape *a Ghetto*—
my exit sealed by the razor of his knuckly
    long finger drawn, lickety-slash,
                across his throat.

Saviour of Assassins

Too soon, three days, six hours, ten minutes after the surrender
        of "the resistance forces"
    and quick takeover of Grenada's seat of government by the invaders,
        arrives in new Port Salinas Airport—
    lauded with much bubbly advance fanfare and pomp—
        sleek private jet of famed British lawyer Gifford, defender
        Czar of outlaws and extremists
      on the political left *or* right. His gunmetal silver
      fuselage shell

sports his laurels, commendatory tall initials burnished—
        in gold script—after his name:
    Q.C., barrister of the elite Queen's Counselors. G's top heavy
        record of trial wins vastly exceeds
    defeats, whose prize stats are touted in the media
      like a champion boxer's unbroken string of first round K.O.'s.
      Within five minutes of Grenada
      jet touchdown, he vows to win freedom and five-figure
      pound sterling

damages for Bishop's slayer—jailed Coard, and his band of thugs;
        though local streetsmarts chatter
    and scuttlebutt cite tall lottery odds that both Coard and cronies
        soon must *hie to the gallows*. At pre-trial
    open forum, grandstand erected slapdash on streetside
      docks at waterfront: dead center of The Carenage, Gifford's
      thrown for a loop by that surprise
      key witness for the prosecution, one gallant frail
      Leslie Pierre,

just-freed political prisoner of some four years "detention,"
            nabbed for editing solo issue
    of *The Voice*, amid earliest months of Bishop's reign in office.
            Gifford, sidestepping L. Pierre's evident
    public appeal, slops out rumsopped loose-tongued case
            against the U.S. spearheaded six nation "plunder" of Grenada's
                "true People's Republic": his key line
            of defense America's gauche political blunder. Free
                speech, free press,

burbles Sir Gifford, flourished in this Spice Isle Democracy
            before the vanguard of overpaid
    mercenaries launched their invasion "assault," barrister's toothy
            bombast soon eclipsed by Pierre's
    plainspoken reply. Thrown into jail without a trial
            nor least semblance of public hearing, the fledgling editor
                joined some five hundred co-inmates:
            the highest Global ratio of political hostages, ever,
                per hundred thousand

citizens, far outstripping Chile's or Argentina's grim record
            of non-criminal arrests, data
    charted by Amnesty International . . . Our legal High Priest, Gifford
            the venerable, is coldly silenced
    by the great wave of applause for Leslie Pierre
            that surges through The Carenage. No let-up. Soon an equal wave
                of hecklers jeers a tottery punch-
            drunk Counselor down from grandstand, to sleep off his Royal
            Gaffe in Jet's bunk.

Names Scrawled on the Priests' Satin Robes

Simeon, among
the first wave of arrests,
    stewed in prison longer than most. Always
    the adept mediator, he kept
    messages on the move between his fellows, and prompted

        secret exchanges, as well,
        with leaders of the underground—ensconced
        in hilltop refuge. Hot word leaked
    to Simeon, first,
           of the impending Human Rights
                Tribunals. America was jockeying to topple
                Bishop's *regime*, or, at the least, to dislodge Maurice
                from his communist allies and cronies,

        the United States, as ever, threatening
        a mightier-than-the-sword dollar pinch. Economic aid
    would be withheld, or worse,
        trade sanctions and boycotts would run amok.
        Bishop, a diplomat of parts, agreed—in principle—to move
    for human rights reform. All parties soon acceded
    to three Tribunal meetings

in neutral State,
Trinidad and Tobago, the chief
    of the commission to be appointed by Bishop.
    Simeon's ear glued to the prison
    floor, window, or latrine stall, got hint of a shocker:

        the rights Tribunal head
        would be Farouk, a Trinidad-born Muslim,
        the most hated prison torturer.

The Tribunal's first
    Council, a team of observers
        from each member country, was deployed
            to inspect prison conditions (a follow-up jury slated
            to target political detainees who

had committed no criminal offense,
    set them apart from trial-court convicted killers, rapists,
assassins, thieves, and make plea
    for their prompt release) . . . As the rights troop
    toured the prison, with stops at every cell, Farouk led
the comings and goings—he monitored all interviews
with prisoners, who feared his wrath

if they stooled—
a wave of never-before-dreamt-of
    beatings, though most inured victims felt braced
    for any punishments bloodthirsty
    Farouk might inflict: worst case, he might—as often before—

    take it out on their wives
    and kids, parents, or brothers and sisters; no few
        would meet with terrible *accidents,*
    gangland style
        mutilations . . . All held their tongues.
            They praised the ghastly prison food, skeletons
            reduced to half their normal weight, denying all charges
            they were underfed (*O shrunken shapes!*);

    praised free flow of medical supplies,
        though sores and pustules from rat bites, spider stings, trickled
down their necks, cheeks and limbs—
    while they demurred all claims of hospital neglect

          as false; declared work hours none too long, nor were inmates
     ever beaten or tortured mercilessly: some jaws and noses
     broken so many times, the swellings

piled up in layers,
arm bones bent into angles beyond
     reckoning, multiple leg-fractures as common
     as nosebleeds; a ghastly style
     of induced bowleggedness, all his own, was mad Farouk's

               personal brandmark. Even so,
          all the victims stayed mum—capitulated. . . .
               Just in recent weeks, the scale
          of debauchery
                    had hit new lows. Two pregnant women,
                         nearing full term when arrested, were forced
                    to give birth in their slimy jail cells, babes christened
                         on the spot; no husband, child, parent

          or other family kin permitted
          to witness either birth or baptizing, the attendant priest
     aghast at the disgrace,
          but he, too, succumbing to coercion and threats;
          the pair of offspring left to face the future, branded thus:
     birthplace, Braxton Prison. Two old men, one dying of liver
     disease, the other cancer,

both demises much
hastened by beatings with clubs
     and rubber hoses: twin sons of the first,
     inmates held in next-door cell,
     endured a sleepless all-night vigil hearing their father's

dying groans and howls, neither
youth given a moment's grace to behold sire
    or minister to his death throes. . . .
The next month,
        when three Roman Catholic priests
            came to jail to render service and sacraments
        for the most devout inmates, the prison warden's guard
            was down. Simeon, joined by a few veteran

cell buddies who'd managed to smuggle
pencil stubs into their clothes, persuaded the clergymen
to let them scrawl the surnames
    plus vital stats of years of government service
    for those many fellow prisoners falsely held in detention
owing to political bias, purely (themselves
included) on the holy scrolls,

bibles, hymnbooks,
even their satin robes; and luckily,
    jail keepers didn't notice the priests staying on
    well beyond the allotted time limits,
    nor espied long lists of names, dates, titles and honors,

        awards scribbled on their collars,
    robe hems, and extended lapels as the churchmen
        sauntered out the gates. Hours later—
    to uttermost
        bafflement of the prison staff—
            key deputies of the rights Tribunal returned,
            without warning, armed with unassailable lists of victims
            lawlessly detained. Thus, Simeon and scores

of his peers and allies were set free,
    a full month prior to Bishop's assassination and the aircraft
  campaign that followed, days later,
    though hundreds of other equally guiltless inmates
      were left behind, among them former judges, doctors, journalists—
all caught on the wrong side of the political fence
before, now hurriedly sent up

to Death Row:
the whole lot of them targeted
    for early hangings, whereby to cover up the worst
    Human Rights violations quick,
      before more rescue sorties by Tribunals spirited them away.

Life Shock: Witness from the Gallows

Wynston is a beacon of liberty, if he
were not in jail, how could we know
that freedom was threatened?
> —Simeon Humphries, Citizen of Grenada

1. *Freedom Spurned*

Within minutes
of his arrival at St. George's
airport, Senator Wynston was rudely frisked
by police, checking for concealed dagger (so they said),
who then thrust a scroll affidavit
under his nose, Wyn's last chance to stay out of prison—
if he would but sign, thus pledging
his support to Bishop; but he flicked away
the pen they offered
with the aplomb of one brushing aside
cobwebs. . . . Handcuffed,
fingerprinted; his assailants flung him
into a crowded cell,
to bed down on pallet straw mat directly beside thrice-
convicted bank heist felon, rapist,
horse thief; Wyn himself leader of the opposition forces
in the Senate, touted as the chief Anti-
Revolutionary, whose jailers
expected to find

him a savage
brute of a man: at six foot five,
two hundred fifty pounds, he was so gentle
and mild-mannered, he disarmed their surly ways. In time,
he became their mentor and ally,
though none would admit this to superior officers; always

seeking his advice—by indirect
questions—about money, physical ills, Romance,
best liquors, herbal
remedies and aphrodisiacs, home repairs:
they were his allured
and adoring students. . . . Yet surprised, he was,
to be sandwiched, cursorily,
between hardened arch criminals, rather than matched up
with other political *resisters*
of his own breed; like most lawful men, the Senator drew
a mental line between outright lawbreakers
and himself. But soon he discerned
the fuzzy line

between convict
and political detainee paled,
melted away. The worst offenders, *three-time
losers,* were often the kindest, most generous cellmates.
One man, uncontrollable arsonist
when at large, was a genius on the guitar, and he wrote
inspired songs to cheer the mates.
Others were gifted drummers, horn players,
who gave their best
sweet talents to the fellows, a loyal
and steadfast band
of chums, always rooting for the underdog
or standing up for the most
downcast among them: the skilled cobbler in the next cell
zestfully patching up everyone's
shoes, making do with the most primitive tools, slipshod
materials—he was a master at recycling
parts of castoff top boots
or throwaway

sandals. Wynston,
himself, gave impromptu lectures
on the arts, stagecraft and Island History,
recited long poems or ballads, then held his listeners
spellbound with tales of old myths
and Carib legends. No wonder, several of the men survived
far better in prison lockup
than after their shock release . . . When the Human
Rights Tribunal folks
visited jail, Wyn hung back, a luminary
who could have saved
himself so easily (if he'd but initialed
the scroll endorsing Bishop,
he walked free), but he rebuffed any hint of favoritism
or privileged status. He deemed
all others in prison as worthy in Spirit as himself,
his near equals under the Higher Law.
Once and for all, he spurned
unreal freedom.

2. *Epidermal Hell*

Every night, for months without letup,
at some mid point between one and two o'clock,
they sprung him out of bed with zaps of an electric prod
to the genitals, then strapped
the Senator into a tall upright seat.
The first time, Wyn surmised it was the electric chair—*his number
was up!* But no, the torturers'
most elegant paraphernalia was reserved

for Citizens of Parts, not to be wasted
　　on your common serial killer, or routine felon.
　　　　At the same hour each night, they woke him from dream reverie
　　　　　　of poems he'd secretly pencilled
　　　　　　　　the day before, yanked him from his cell
　　half-drugged with sleep, and strapped him in his oversize Throne,
　　　　high metal chair back matched
　　to his lengthy frame, a man six foot five

in his better days—now bowed over, shrunk
　　some few centimeters, no less; and the ghastly art
　　　　of inducing pain without limit commenced. . . . Chinese Rubber
　　　　　　Torture, that classy import
　　　　　　　　from the prisons of Peking, kept
　　eight steps ahead of even their Siberian counterparts in State-
　　　　of-the-Art torture hardware.
　　Three rubber hammers, released in sync, began

thudding upon his body: one hammer
　　slugged his forehead from above, while two others
　　　　battered each of his hands. Taps of the flat-edged hammers,
　　　　　　travelling at slow speeds
　　　　　　　　across a short arc, seemed mild enough,
　　at first. He even grew to anticipate each next hammer's clap
　　　　with a weird martyr's pleasure
　　　　(*if this is their worst, I welcome it, O keep*

it coming), but after an hour or two,
　　the oddly seductive rhythm took a lethal turn.
　　　　Only three skin patches were engaged, directly, but he felt
　　　　　　as though every square inch
　　　　　　　　of his flesh—even the dry sockets

under his arms, the damp pouch that tightly clamped his balls—
caught the same agonizing sting,
as from thousands of poison needles piercing

his body's rind, at once (*so this is it,*
now I'm halfway to hell, what's next?): epidermal
surface, in its entirety, seemed to have been translated
into a pore-lined organic
pin cushion. . . . But at some incalculable
moment, each night, his psychic gears swerved, shifted within him
as he wriggled this way and that,
tugging at his straps. It may be he sought

an inner counter rhythm to oppose to
the deathly glum monotone of the rubber hammers.
Perhaps he found himself, at those junctures, planning lines
for his next morning's poem,
stuttering the key words he might fasten
around images. It's certain that he bellowed, at intervals—sang out
syllables! And do you know, the sound
of word chants roared in his dulled ears saved him.

3. *Smuggled Pencil Stubs*

Wyn's best
poems, written secretly
and forbiddenly in prison, came sallying forth
in a great rush
during those last four days on Death Row, following the murder
of Maurice Bishop. . . . Though he was shrewd enough
to keep his verses hidden from the prison guards, scrawled
on toilet paper
or scraps of linen, they knew he was up to something. So they went

to sadistic
loony extremes to baffle
Senator Wynston, to trick him into believing
his brain was zapped.
There was not the remotest trace of light in Solitary Pit,
so little basis, then, for him to guess
the time of day, much less how many days were passing;
but to disorient
him still more, his jailers, thinking he guessed time by arrival

of such paltry
meals as they dispensed,
shuffled the schedule, delaying one meal by an extra
half day, then serving
the next an hour later, never following the same time lapse
pattern twice in succession. And it worked.
He grew oblivious to time of day, didn't know a day's
from a week's passage.
Even in those last weeks before Bishop's assassination, when Wyn

was sent down
to Death Row, they started
to noticeably tighten the screws on the Senator—
what had they to fear
from him, a helpless tottering skeleton of the man he'd been?
Perhaps they could sense the elation of heart
and spirit his poems had burgeoned, but they could never
have surmised the source:
his creative scribblings were too well concealed, the papery snippets

tucked away
in thin knife-blade slits
of his fiber mattress. He was allowed to receive

visits from family
for brief stints, but only if he was docile and subservient.
Should he try—as was even his sleep daze bias!—
to discuss philosophy or religion, much less politics,
with any of the guards
or fellow prisoners (they eavesdropped on him at all hours, to run

periodic checks
on his irrepressible bouts
of bombast and rant), they'd cut him off without meals
altogether, then turn
away his would-be visitors, saying he was too sick or distraught
to see anyone. And today, those inanities
loom largest in his fading memory of worst final weeks
of prison life. Even then,
his poems, which he recited in whispers to himself, gave him constant

succor. . . . Prison,
it seemed, had sprung the poet
from the political animal. His art life began
as wordless visions,
dreams of romance and freedom, yet he'd always startled back
from the intensest free flights of spirit
to the fatal chill of his blank prison walls. And now,
he rekindles those surges
of rhapsodic discovery: "Oh, how much we take for granted unearned

daily givens,
when free. To witness Nature,
fish, birds, trees in the gale, stars on a clear night,
all these cost-free
gifts, most precious, precious, be taken from us by prison walls."
But despite the deprivations numberless, he felt,

absurdly, nothing was lost: there is *no dying, no dying,*
    except death of the Soul.
As never before, his free spirit felt limitlessly alive and awake.

      His first poem,
    "I am awake," erupted whole
  from a hauntingly beautiful recurrent dream.
    Whenever he drifted off
to sleep, his dormant self *came to,* robustly, in the dreamscape,
  chanting, *I'm awake, I'm awake.* He'd memorized
the six brief verses, and kept murmuring this upbeat refrain
    over and over in cell dark,
when grief or rage or pain seemed to be nullifying him. Ah, the poem's

    strange energy
  and unfailing power lifted
him from the slump of despondency. No doldrums
    could sink him for long.
He composed other poems, one by one, reciting the whole slow-
  growing repertoire to himself, his verbal powers
of improvisation blooming richer the more he exercised
    his gifts; much as Messiaen,
while incarcerated in Nazi labor camp, wrote his unearthly classic

    chamber work,
  Quartet for the End of Time,
highlighting the birdlike voice of the clarinet.
    Though Wyn's gravest loss
had been his body's utter severance from the world of Nature,
  since he was never permitted to lay one foot
outdoors, his senses magically recovered what his body
    had lost—in time, he learned
to hear the very air currents gusting around him sing. The breezes

that swirled
all about his cell bespoke
wonders to him, no stopping those gale force winds
from blowing through wall
vents; while more and more, he trained himself to differentiate
a wide range of bird warbles, mouse squeaks, rabbit
and chipmunk stutters, diverse scents of pollens, flowers,
changing, however subtly,
with the flux of seasons. They gave voice to his heightened pickup.

Never before
had he known such alertness,
such receptivity, to Nature's every slow nuance
as now—which was transmitted
to him at the caprice or fine whimsy of the companionable gusts
(didn't his jailers guess his joy? no way to squelch
free flow of Carib trade winds). . . . But in his dark moments,
it was an agony to Wyn
to have his head be buzzing and effervescing with keenest messages,

yet no paper
or pencil to transcribe verses
that invaded his ear more quickly than he could hope
to retain them by heart,
though he'd already committed to memory some hundreds of lines.
At last, his friends outside conspired to wangle
pencil stubs to his cell, where he cunningly hoarded strips
of toilet paper and tagends
of bed linen—and thereon, he scratched his piecemeal & bounteous song.

4. *Life Shock*

Prime Minister Bishop was under House Arrest, just three days
after he was *detained.*
      Casual talk—between the Cuban
officers—turned,
more and more, to betting odds that he'd be executed
      before this hectic week
wound down. Never *if*, but *when,* he'd be shot, in public,
with open guile and bravado
      of presiding Generalissimos. They muttered,
      freely, of the impending
assassination,

        within easy earshot of Senator Wynston, as well as the other
                      twenty-two political
        inmates on Death Row: "They counted you
             among THE DEAD
    already, and indeed, you felt that you were listening
        to all such barbarous threats
    through boards of your coffin. Maurice Bishop's slaughter
        was followed by so grave a hush,
      the bloody event itself seemed like a dream,
          an unreal afterthought. . . . We'd
             never heard a clue

about the invasion, days later. So we assumed all the uproar,
bombs going off and small-arms
      gunfire, was momentary Civil War:
a spontaneous
uprising of diehard Bishop loyalists, old faithfuls
      soon to be quashed by Cuban

strongmen. Six hours before we were tagged, at two-minute
intervals, to hang from the Gallows,
     our jail gates burst open: we were set free!
     Old-time friends hoisted us
upon their shoulders

       and paraded us down the avenues. . . . *We were ash-faced ghosts.*
                    Our reprieve was a sad joke
          we couldn't fathom, or accept—for months,
                    only SLOW DEATH
         of four prison years seemed real. You, a traveler, know
             frequent culture shock. But this
       was LIFE SHOCK. We were afflicted, we felt, with the virus
               of corpse-stunned-alive syndrome.
       My head was under water, or stuffed with balls
             of cotton—though for all
               the world, to family,

dear ones, I may have seemed my old pure self again. *Outwardly.*
I was immersed in sleepwalker's
     trance, a choking-without-loss-of-breath
sensation, when
the U.S. State Department chaps came to call at my flat.
     They cheered me at the door
with pretense of a hero's welcome that I'd learned, by now,
to ignore. It was already too late.
     Brainwashed, they were, by unctuous counselors
     and moneyed aristocrats. Oh, all
my raspy-throated words

flew past them: they should take leads from *men in the street*,
                              those ordinary working-class
               citizens who, by the thousands, showered
                                   their love and thanks
upon your Marines when they bounded onto piers; our local
                  Belles, wild for the American
uniforms, thinking naught could be sweeter than to be seen
                         hugging a U.S. Marine, cap off,
       sleeves rolled up for the cameras, shaking crewcut
                   in shock and disbelief at—yes!—
                              the ardent fierce welcome."

The Ballad of Garfield John

for Dave Smith

1.

    Dining, solo,
  in the outdoor back gallery of Toulouse
seaside French Bistro, I notice a youth seated, cross-
      legged, back
  to a palm, on the sandy beach. He peruses
a magazine in his lap. Dressed in jeans and cotton flower-
      print shirt,
  long and lanky, he springs to greet me
at the exit gate. *At your service,* says he. *Anythinyasay.*
    No problem.
  Garfield John. Garfield the cat soldier.
Earned his title by staging many a successful ambush:
    working alone,
  he'd pounce on squads of invading troops,
dispersing their ranks. Maestro of the element of surprise,
    Garfield kept
  them off balance. Did the enemy one better.
Like the back of his hand, he knew slight dips and hummocks
    of the terrain,
  could turn on a dime: he'd challenge their guns,
they'd drop their gun belts (*O I sent them running for cover,*
    many a time),
  whose whirlwind quickness of eye and agility
of prance was second to none in his local top-flight platoon.
    Most painful
  to recall, Garfield witnessed two dear pals
slain in combat; his eyes glaze over, when he narrates details
    of woundings,

himself shot twice (fear he might bleed
to death quickly squelched, when he dragged a leg-crushed
        sweet comrade
    to safety)—*feel here,* says he, and I do,
my fingertip tracing the wide perimeters of scarred gouge
        in his underbelly.
    No way could he dodge or avert that hit
by a crooked spear of exploded mortar shell. He's lucky
        it didn't slice
    him in two! How strange it was to unwind,
slowly, the long jagged-edged icicle from his hemorrhaging
        gut: amazed,
    even now, to think of his cool and steady hand
as he worked the mammoth sliver of castiron this way and that
        about his innards
    to free it from whatever organs it embraced
so madly, the pain, excruciating though it was from the start,
        seemed to belong
    to another corpus—none of his own bloodied
entrails peeping out, but a friend's. *I must help my brother,*
        he'd chanted,
    in stupor, as he kept twisting—O so gently!—
that spiral-curved foreign body loose from his lower bowel.
        Today, in dreams,
    he relives his gut's fantastic disimpalement,
the metal shard imaged as a giant corkscrew. Many a nightmare
        finds him puffing
    and grinding at his midsection to get unskewered. . . .
As we chat, the last of twilight fades away from our stretch
        of rocky coastline,
    then slinks quickly across the bay, and bores
into Horizon's burrow like a snake whipping into its channel.

2.

I ask after deep shrapnel pocks on Garfield's
forearm, whether he feels much pain from the lumps
of metal still lodged in two subcutaneous
zones, or suffers some loss of function. He shakes

his head, *Nay.* . . . "In first hours of surprise assault,
mortar shells were falling everyplace at once,
the smoke so thick from that spate of falling flak
and showers of flamy debris bestrewn
by the firestorm of government buildings ablaze,
no familiar landmarks could be trusted—
shattered road tarmac and the frequent craters

threw our ground map out of whack. We couldn't know
where in the Hell we were standing, squatting or creeping,
from one moment to the next. Your U.S. Marines,
I must say, were *awesomely* well-trained,

since those bumbling dunderheads, infantry hacks
from the *Misbegotten Six* island regiments,
could never have staged any landing whatsoever
without the superior crack battalion
of Marine frontrunners leading the charge, who won
immediate foothold at Grand Anse Beach
and held that beachhead throughout the crucial hours

of all Eastern Carib-bloc troop landings." Granted,
the U.S. Marine Squad's advance spearhead
stole his awe and emulation, but his lips curl
pixieish grin as he recalls the slapdash

lies and distortions of the Clint Eastwood movie
Heartbreak Ridge, which projected the whole four-days-war
as bloodless coup, mere child's play, an easy rout
of the few Cuban guerrillas ("dumb renegades
and outlaws—what a farce!") by our hero Marine
Rambos . . . "Not a true frame in the two-hours-long
propaganda flick! I was there, I tell you,

and I saw dozens of Americans slaughtered
in ten minutes, maybe one hundred more wasted
in that first hour. As for the purported lone Cuban
stragglers of the enemy forces your *Freedom*

Allies faced, most Cubans I'd known dropped their guns
and walked away from the fracas. It's true, some
Cubans loved to have the official alibi
to kill U.S. soldiers, and they shot plenty,
but the fiercest warriors were Grenadian
locals like myself, fighting in THE RESISTANCE,
mad to make any sacrifice! We'd have fought

cannons with our bare hands, if need be, to uphold
our small nation's sovereignty (for two hundred years,
without fail, staunch defenders of our shores
against pirates, barbarians, and so-called

colonizers) . . . My immediate small troop
boasted three of the meanest vigilantes I've
ever beheld at work on uniformed human
meat—carcasses plastered wherever they set foot!
One fearless tiger of a gunslinger, ex-
farmboy from the nutmeg and allspice plantations,
Reynaldo—whom we nicknamed *Terminator*—

took out two whole St. Lucian and Barbadian
squads, in separate charges. I saw him brawling
singlehandedly, without backup; but tell that, sir,
to the few survivors at the outermost fringe

of the marauder's wide orbit, who escaped
with multiple flesh wounds, at best, so convinced
were they that they must be outnumbered, since rifle
fire seemed to come at them from everyplace
at once. And so many close buddies were crumpling
around them, they each had hurdles of fallen
kinsmen to trip over as they hightailed

it out of there like wild fox or billy goat,
I never saw men gallop so fast outside
the Olympics on TV, but believe me,
Reynaldo was the sole scourge of PUMPKIN HILL!

Truly, he looked like a Halloween Demon,
and likewise, the curved trench halfway up the bluff
where, hid in dugout, he lay perched for ambush,
resembled a Jack-O-Lantern's wide-toothed
grin. Fiery glows pulsing in hill sockets above,
where gouges had been dug by early mortar
shells, might be the pumpkin's eyes. Those Ammo

flashes kept groaning through magazine chambers
of his twin automatic rifles, one gun tucked
under each arm, as he LORDLY unloaded
a dozen stuffed cartridge belts into advancing

infantries. From below, where I crouched
in the trench opposite, the rifle flash did seem
to surge through eyes, nose and mouth of a great MOON
FACE: a man-eating furnace of fire, the pumpkin's
vengeful fury at the invaders! Clumped piles
of men were eaten alive, every three minutes,
by our Reynaldo's famed two-handed dual

marksmanship. But I repeat, the Pumpkin Hill
Massacre was all the savage handiwork
of one man, not the supposed SWAT team of twenty
a few survivors reported back to their beach

encampment had knocked out both waves of the hill-charge
squadron. And Reynaldo would've kept mowing down
whole armies 'til daybreak, if lucky sniper
bullets hadn't nailed him. Or perhaps, his own platoon
mate's accidental stray crossfire, it's rumored,
got him, since the enemy troops had no access
to his hideaway burrow. . . . Worse yet, the bloodstorms

of "Pit Viper" Wang Chu, the baddest sharpshooter
in memory, who blew away twice Reynaldo's
number of war dead in a prolonged orgy
of incineration back in the valley. Fierce Wang Chu,

Chinese Trinidadian, was leader of that band
of well-paid mercenaries from Trinidad—
the one East Caribbean country, you'll remember,
which firmly opposed the invasion. Master
Wang, it was, who trained our special tactics unit
of Grenadians, my hard-bitten teenage mates
and myself. Wang, the unvanquished, never fell

prey to our enemy's last barrage of merged flanks,
forces two thousand strong. Stowaway in deep ballast
hold of prominent family's fishing vessel,
he now safely enjoys his ex-soldier-Jock hero's

status, quite publicly, in Port-of-Spain,
Trini's Capitol. But I'll spare you grim bod count
of his record number *Enemy Kills* (no fewer
than half were American, though World Press be sworn
to secrecy: fake coverup), since you, YANKEE,
accept—without question—your State Department's
scandalous lie: ONLY NINETEEN U.S. CASUALTIES."

3.

      I take the brief pause, hiatus
in Garfield's Four-Days'-War Saga, to query his case for Cuba's
      good will mission for Grenada's future. "Oh,
          that news media rubbish!"
he replies: "Vast stockpiles of Cuban arms and munitions

      camouflaged in the secret woods
fortress: it was all faked by those State Department stooges,
      a put-up job. I knew that patch of terrain
          like my family's homestead;
the whole area was void of supplies, or fortifications,

      one day before the troop landings—
strictly a frameup, a slipshod one at that. Any honest newsman
      worth his salt could've spotted the obvious
          telltale marks of forgery.
It was a shambles, a botchup, mostly Korean or Taiwanese

cheap firearms *planted* in plain view
(no search team could miss the burlap sacks of guns and grenades
    in the first ten minutes foraging through brush),
        a feeble job of hideaway
at best, most simpleminded case of a setup you ever saw.

    No Cuban or Grenadian soldiers
I'd hobnobbed with would be caught dead packing such obsolete
    or defective arms. We knew the best weapons
        on sight, trained to espy
the shoddy makes, and none of those stockpiled brands

    bore the imprint of the genuine
article. I examined them myself, displayed in St. George's public
    square, the day after our RESISTANCE FORCES'
        defeat. Likewise, I'm sure
they faked the leaflets, papers with plans of a four-

    stage Cuban takeover of the farms,
schools and economy . . . Letting me and my local comrades-in-arms
    go scot-free, that's quite a joke on the Marine
        Dead: too easy, it was,
for us teenage Commandos to pretend we were manhandled,

    terrorized—by torture and death
threats to our families—to join forces with Cuban *Generalissimos*
    against the invading troops; but I stayed mum
        about the crap third-rate
guns and ammo, since I wanted to keep my lowest profile,

    quietly on the sidelines. I saw
plenty of knowing smirks on the faces of war veteran pressmen,
    no pushovers when it came to junk guns, worm-eaten

riflestocks, tinny off-center
gunsights. I tell you anyone half-initiated could detect

fake weapons, but no press crews
wanted to seem unpatriotic, or tarnish the success of Reagan's
vaunted Carib rescue; so the World Press Club—
a global conspiracy, of sorts—
choked down the truth, looking the other way. I could

have smashed those warp-grained
gunstocks over my knee like so many tomato plant stakes, or kite
crossbars. So be it! I, too, held my tongue—
for shame . . . U.S. State Dept.
goons will forge, steal or defraud on the least pretext. . . ."

"But you digress. What of alleged
pure motives of the Cubans?" I taunt. "None came to be soldiers,"
Garfield snaps back. "They were simple craftspeople
and technicians, here to build
roads and the new Point Salinas Airport, working side-by-side

with my brothers and cousins, uncles,
in peace and harmony, employed by the Grenada Public Works Dept.
Men and woman of good will, hardworking souls, our
helpmates, they came to Grenada
to do an honest job, collect their meager wages and return

to Cuba, none the wealthier for it.
The Cuban workfolks, vast numbers crammed in truck-square fuselage
like herds of cattle, many youths I grew to love
as friends among them,
were deported back to Havana in wide-bodied transport planes."

4.

Just after dusk,
    we take a short drive through coast hills
to Garfield's valley house, he wishing to don his *spiffy duds*
        for this night's
    jump-up dance on Loveboat Wharf. En route
he praises the new low-rent housing projects, scores of prefab
        wall units piled
    beside the road, a building trend he credits
to the Americans (so to make amends, having scolded my derelict
        political animal,
    brute country of my birth); in the next breath,
he finds himself trying to justify those many recent muggings
        of foreigners,
    we Americans in particular: "If anyone *deserves*
to get ripped off here, the Yankees are fair game!" No reply.
    Moments later,
    after a token shift of topic: "Perhaps, Bud,
you can see yur way clear to loan me a small piece-a-change,
        piece-a-change."
    Still no answer. He tugs me near, confers
the honor of divulging some top-secret up-to-the-minute info,
        thereby to earn
    easy money handout he keeps jockeying for:
"The Revolution, here, dormant for a time, is far from stifled.
        Rebel forces
    are building. We'll spring back to power
within months. Do keep it under your hat." I promise, by finger
        gesture, *my lips*
    be sealed. And I pay for three small candles
to light his hut, and then wait in the car, admiring the nightglow
        in hilltop acres

above Port City. By glimmer of a single wick's
pulse, he undresses—the ceiling lower than his upright frame,
  his candle throws
 a wriggly stooped shadow from roof window,
and I picture him crouching into his shirt and pants, his voice,
  warm and ardent,
 springing out to me on a wave of spontaneous
good feeling: "How are you loving that fine moonlight out there?"
  Snuffs his candle.
 Emerges, smelling fresh as wild mountain roses.
O he disarms me of all caution, tinged with shame, as I swallow
  my cowardly fear
 of Garfield who, guileless, hums and chants
anthems for revival of *Our Revolution.* . . . Now we speed downhill
  to floodlit pier,
 where Loveboat dancers are in full swing
alongside the bay waters, the dock all one long dance platform.

 III

Eastern
Caribbean
Medley

Cudjoe's Head

Six old gaffers, perched on roadside poles, smirk—
perhaps they silently mock the surprise in my face
upon first hearing the origin of their village's name:

                         CUDJOE'S HEAD, where,
          with much festive hoopla,
            a runaway slave's head was hacked off
by masked officer
      wielding a machete. . . .
        The Northside wing of this Island's
        an ongoing lesson
in history, echoed by local place names.
We're parked at a summit, of sorts, smallish hilltop
          between two ravines—
           steep gullies that once held pools
   or shallow rivers:

today, they revert—if rarely—to whirling waters
when heaviest rains hit the twin peaks of nearby Cross's
Point Mountain, flooding the area. The deeper canyon,

                  below town center,
        half-shrouded by thickets,
        coppice & natural contours of hillside,
is RUNAWAY GHAUT.
   This narrow valley
        served as hideaway and escape
        chute, by turns,
for those splinter troops of fugitive slaves
making a dash between workshifts, eluding armed wardens
          of their Plantation
          Estates. So few flocks of fieldhands
   absconded to safe

retreat and sanctuary in adjacent forest (a mere paucity
of bold rebels amid thousands of cowed sheep), their absence
was hardly noticed. But when the youngest offspring

                              in a fleetfooted
            slave family of runaways,
                himself a portly laggard, was trapped
by the deputy guard
        at gorge mouth—his parents
            and siblings long since withdrawn
                from view—Cudjoe
was beheaded on the spot with high public
ceremony, to discourage future breakouts: loose skull
                oddly hurtled
                down the canyon, as if chasing
        his nimbler kinsfolk. . . .

House Walk over the Mountain

for Michael Madonick

Still in his late
teens, already twice a father,
    Willock built his house in the arid Province
    of Porches—planed every board,
    hit every nail himself. He'd won permission from Chief

                Forest Ranger
                Quinn to cut three cedar timbers from densely wooded
Chance's Peak, subdivided
    all board feet for his home from that prized
        trio of logs, and salvaged every limb, branch, or twig
    for window frames, lintel, sill . . .
Cotton crops slow to mature in Porches' drought,
    Willock saved up his pence two years, earning down payment

    rental on one land *contour* in soil-rich Whites.
      Then, he launched
          his six-mile uphill trek, fine-tooled leak-proof-
            roofed squarish house jacked up
          on a low steel trailer frame, held aloft by ten trundle
    wheels; and with two teams of horses, one donkey,

pulling the front end,
he and his three chums half-pushed,
    half-guided, the bob-and-pitch house back end
    for the entire pothole-gouged
    stretch of roadway. They felt like displaced landlubber

           Tritons madly
          flailing about, wrenching the baseboard this way and that,
as if jostling to steer
      a great ship's hull from the stern in typhoon
        gales; repeatedly, a wheel or two slid off the road
      edge, great weight of a corner block
crumbling the shelf of embankment, small avalanche
        unleashed—the house tilted, teetery on the overhang, poised

      over the gulch below. But always, they wobbled
      the edifice, slowly,
         back to upright position, hauling those stout
           guideropes for all their barefooted
         worth (in gravel sunk-to-the-ankles), the shaky domicile
      thus saved from certain collapse into piecemeal

firewood and splinters
on the ravine's rock-jaggedy
      banks. . . . *See for yourself,* says Willock. *There stands
      she, a full sixty-two years later
      none the worse, in all her tin-roofed and rustproof Glory!*

In Fear of the Music Scholar

For some months now,
    village fledgling spell
        charmers, novices in voodoo
        and lesser rites,
glare at David Shaw. Wordless, they accuse,
accuse—he *suspect* among them. Rumor hoopla nails him
        a voodoo High Priest,
          master of black magic arts and rites.
    Many street yokels
      scoff at his shy denials.
        Two dabblers in Haitian voodoo,
          recent newcomers to Statia from Fort-
du-France, Martinique,

overhear Shaw
    in Sunday morning church
        services: the pair ensconced,
        hunchingly stooped
low, in pew behind him, while he chants
quietly under his breath during a brief hiatus, or pause
        in lengthy High Mass.
        Shaw unawares, no clue to eavesdroppers,
    hums and recites,
      by turns, verses he'd first
        learned in childhood, brief snatches
        of liturgy, which, if caught by alien ears,
resemble the melange

of Christian
    and ghostly incantation
        oft muttered in Haitian voodoo
        chants (bastardized,

but kept loosely intact, in Guadeloupe
or Martinique spinoffs); suspicion doubled, since Shaw's
         French accent and dialect
         so closely matches theirs. That, alone,
     brands him wizardly
       and spooky, this whitehaired
         nocolor bloke who spent years
         of his life—prior to Statian wedlock—
in study and music

research in Fort-
     du-France, their home base,
       though neither back-bent Frenchie
       can guess Shaw's real
kinship to them. Too late, near the finish
of his private recital, he glimpses the pair of snoops
         and alters his song—
         too late! From that morn, rumor thickly
     spreads that David's
       a demonic shaman: voodoo
         High Priest. Thence, he's shunned
         in street and market square by stranger
and friend, alike,

each guarded soul
     keeping a strict remove,
       or divide, from befuddled Shaw,
       as if a potent
circle of just-sprinkled satanic powders
surrounds his person, the noxious aura wafting in step
         with him as he walks,
         trots, stoops to sample wares; or chats,

wryly, with neighbor
    child, perhaps whistling
        at domestic pet—fowl, goat, mutt. . . .
        He conjectures the pair of French youths
may have touched off

his defamation.
    One night, he queries them
        in a bar: tight on beers, loose-
        tongued, they spill
the charge against him, for fear he'll cast
deathly spell upon them. How could he know those verses
        recited in unearthly
        French accent? He sighs: *I learned them,*
    at age seven, in Church
        of Christ: bilingual French
        and Anglo, in my Rhode Island home
        parish. . . . Slowly, word gets out—exculpates *low*
priest of song books.

White Tiger and the Mosquitoes

From Tortola to St. Kitts, I encounter
hard-working proud parents
of aviators: doubling up nights
and weekends—
moonlighters at those second
and third jobs—to send
their sons (today, a few daughters,
as well) to the famed school for Master Pilots
in Trinidad. My cab driver,
Guyana-born, brags about prowess
of his rugged pilot son, touting his top-of-the-line
job prospects. . . . In mid Sixties
Grenada, he tells me, careers in piloting
hit their acme.

This small nation produced more superior
pilots, per capita,
than any other country—*worldwide.*
It was, without a doubt, the *in ting* for most Grenadian
lads: *if the glamour puss*
local chicks heard that you were going to fly,
mon, you were at least halfway home with them! . . .

Tough old Captain Farfan, veteran of twice
daily non-stop flights
from London to Port-of-Spain, heads
the Trinidad
Master Classes for all pilot
trainees. The students,
he complains, are—with few exceptions—
lax and inattentive, though their roster includes
only Top Gun apprentice

pilots from aviation prep schools
throughout the Caribbean. Hah, they swerve bolt upright
in their seats when Cap Farfan
(retired Commander of the British RAF)
spins his yarns—

mostly true, drawing on facts of his life—
about his many combat
missions flown solo over *Deutschland*
in the Great War. But they fall back to slouch and dawdle
mode whenever he resumes
the daily lessons. Since the students know him
for a sixth-generation Trini man, proud scion

of one of the earliest British settler's
families, why—he asks me—
do they fight him *every fool step*
of help's way?,
resist or repulse his sly
hard-bitten tricks
of the trade, secret knacks he learned
on-the-run, installed behind the control panels
during strafer attack missions.
Or dogfights. His whitish skin hue,
it may be, undermines his sway with them, though often
he boasts, coyly, that he pumps
20% African blood through these nose-diver
old tiger grit

loop-the-loop arteries and veins, and indeed,
to illustrate his point,
he holds his breath & chug chugs
in place until his neck and forehead veins bulge purply—

but Black is *pure Black.*
And the chaps won't settle for skin color pranks
      or recessive-gene Race quibbles. . . . One day, Farfan

brings his cocoa-skinned sixty-year-old
    "kid" sister to class.
        But nobody believes *she be same*
          family kin.
        For too long, they know him
        WHITE TIGER Farfan,
      no relenting, now, on their *bleach face*
    visage of him. . . . How he loves to rehash his lowdown
      on the old primitive fighter
        planes he flew in The War: levers jammed,
          pedals stuck, you had to get down on your hands & knees
        in mid flight (putting your wheel
          on an improvised hanger device, that gimmick
          he'd cooked up

      in lieu of today's automatic pilot), grubbing
about, this way and that,
    in the steamy rumblebox bowels
      of the cockpit: kick pipes with your boot, slam floorboards
    with a hammer when engines
missed a few beats—threatened a mortal stallout.
    It was rather like stoking a steel smelter's blast

furnace that's lost its spark. You had to get
    those pump-driven pistons
      going again in fractions of a sec,
        or risk DEATH
        DIVES: *it's no fun to bail out*

over Nazi line
encampments, let me tell you . . . Survivor
skills! You had to keep up your daily calisthenics,
   so much more sinew and burly
      muscle at the ready was needed
         to keep those machines greased and primed: if an engine
            was fussy, a prop gone cranky,
               fixing to kick out, you had to hear it, catch
                  first warning

         signals, then stomp hell out of those fuel pipes,
and wring the hoses' necks
      before they cut their flow of juice
         with your bare hands—or asbestos gloves, if you'd the time
      and gumption to be getting
those heavy mitts on your paws before the freeze
      hit the lines. . . . And none ever doubted his tales

about two abortive near-crash night landings
   behind enemy lines.
         Mid winter cold. Freezing sleet
            to be whisked
               from windshields & tail vent
         cables, one wing's
            flaps ice-jammed . . . Our Farfan landed
on-a-dime in a three-acre woods clearing, managed
   the minor repairs in few minutes
      before the local militias found him,
         good Cap a master of the skip-and-jump hopscotch takeoff:
            three shakes of his trusty wood prop,
               he'd be airborne once more . . . *O forget about*
                  raging war

conditions, today's pilots needn't be skilled
Ace jiffy repairmen
   into the peacetime flyer's bargain,
     only one prime artistry's all ye need master in our day:
    PILOTING, 'n that's too much
for you slackoff tenderfeets! . . . Cap's favorite
     aircraft, *bar none,* were the all wood carved-block

   small Mosquito bombers. In them, he flew dozens
    of multi-strike missions
      back in the German hinterlands,
       knocking out
       whole supply truck cordons
      & munitions fleets
       as they sped down shrouded dirt roadways
     to the front lines. He loved best keen fragrances
      of those differing hardwoods,
        so kept all moving parts well-oiled
        and polished himself. How could he trust the hack rookie
        Air Force mechanics to service
         his rosy-hued gleamy-paneled craft? He unpacked
         and repacked

     the housings, next wrapt the pipes & cylinders
with moist cloths to protect
   fine woods from overheating or cracking;
     asbestos fireproofing layers wound tightly over the bulks,
   then puffing fire-resistant
sprays to enhance the natural sturdy seal
    of the inborn resins, as prescribed by diagrams

in manuals and service charts. . . . To hold forth
   upon natural beauties
      of old wood MOSQUITOES was, to Farfan,
         Lyric Verse,
         and he seemed to operatize
      old Norse Poesy
      when he chanted to his dazed students
   the quaint litanies: namings of aeronautical parts,
      routines for best daily upkeep
         and mellow wood tone. The war plane
            might have been a cross between your antique Stradivarius
            violin and a world's champion
         racehorse, for all Farfan's polysyllabic
            locutions

            of tranced recital. . . . One time, Cap was shot down:
a man in his late twenties
   who'd flown dozens of strafing missions
      in great battles of Malta and World War II without ever once
   taking a hit to his wing,
tail, or fuselage; but this mortar shell caught
      him in rear dead center, carved his whole tail section

   clean off, much like a sardine-can opener
      chisels away the flat top
         panel of tin, all-of-a-piece.
            Oh, he knew
            in an instant what he'd lost!
         All steering cables
         and landing gear hookup had been voided
      from his control stick at once, the warning signals
         blinking on his dashboard, alarms

buzzing—he bent forward, one last time,
to kiss the sepias and pale maroons of that crown prince
assemblage of old woods,
then checked his chute fasteners & bailed out,
just before

the Mosquito's nose went into irreversible
downthrust . . . He fell to earth
three miles behind the front lines,
not far from eye range of sentry or trenches, and hid out
in thick brush; then he dug
himself a bodypit in earth (mock gravesite,
he fancied), popped out a few minutes each night

to scoop up roots and drink from rain puddles,
lapping water like a puppy
to save time—back to his shallow ditch.
He'd snap awake,
between naps, to a mixed chorus
of bombers overhead
(his pilot fellows) and anti-aircraft
shellings. . . . The students may well have perked up
on their stools to challenge
his story's last chapter, the escape
saga—how he eluded, finally, those German pursuers
aided by their bloodhounds, flares,
teargas bombs and flame throwers. But when,
purportedly,

he crossed the borders into occupied Malaysia,
negotiated all checkpoints
with overt brashness of public display,

and passed freely out the heavily guarded exit turnstiles
to *The Free World*, who can fail
to mock his word portrait of himself as dressed
in the sarong and headdress of a native Malay. . . .

"Farfan, you are so tall and lightskinned,
wrong body type, odd shape
altogether," we cavil, this night,
over cocktails.
Without delay, our pilot flaps
out of his easy chair—
wordless, mute before us detractors—
and zips from the parlor, returning in six minutes:
his lengthy physique now wound,
smartly, in a bed sheet full-body
sarong, three hand towels wrapped in a passably colorful
head kerchief, pot belly
and hip spread masked by drapery of skirt kilts
as he rises

to full height, and struts across the gallery,
tossing off a few slangy
dialect phrases with quick tongue rolls.
Lastly, he places a large flower pot atop the headdress
and sweeps it about the room
with utmost balance—surety of neck poise to fool
us all, and a gaggle of goosestepping Nazis, to boot.

Wharf Angel

5 A.M. Friday.
My second full day in St.
Martin. Up at daybreak, I miss out
on sweet balcony
Main Street overlook,
petit dejeuner breakfast,
to hop minibus
from French Marigot to Dutch Sint Maarten,
then reserve a space on *Style* speedboat for Tuesday's
once-a-week jaunt
to volcanic Saba. . . . I ramble down six
or seven docks,

hunting the Harbor
Master for ticket purchase—
too early perhaps; I drop to a squat,
braced for the vigil.
Soon a long-legged,
bouncy commanding figure sweeps
from a dockhouse,
sandaled, mustachioed, tall . . . O happiest
presence! More gull than man, arms so freely swung
at his sides,
they could be disguised wings,
pinions tucked

under underarms.
I can barely discern knit
shirt, or his skin-tight diaphanous
pants—he's so shorn
of garb, deadmass of duds.
I ask directions to the Saba

ferryboat, *Style.*
Stay put, says he. An earlybird dockhand
will arrive soon, who takes *cash only* for passage,
    no tickets, mind you.
      Scrawled receipt's good as currency.
  My informant,

        SKYJACK (his moniker
    chanted by transient chums),
      seems carved from stout cedar planks
of this very wharf,
    no crack or warp anyplace.
      Now I ask after his livelihood.
      Charters cruises. Works
alone. His *own* boat. All sails extempore,
unplanned. No advance reservations. No distances
      too short, nor too far;
      no time limits; no fixed rates:
  all's settled

        in a quick word
      between pards, mate. Mate, he
    calls me, and I like the feel of it,
try on that name
    like a lifejacket at sea,
      it fits snug and lightweight;
      gladly, I'd trade
some few other names I don't much need
to be Skyjack's mate for a stretch, I whimsy. *Pray.*
    But not aloud.
      Ah, how his world speaks from him,
  this man wedded

                    livelong to his ship.
          Like my blossoming apricot
          tree last spring, he unfolds flower
world unto himself,
     luminescence: a seed
          blown from soil to soil, takes root
          in any turf,
some manship airplant at home in all winds,
all seas. So here is a lean knobby burgeoned tree
                    of a tallish man,
          who becomes the more *rooted*
     the more he flails

                         away from all bounds
          of territory; and blooms
          the more for all his easy command
and grip of yardarms:
     no salesman, no procurer
          of wares, who he is he offers,
          gives of himself
freely, to any taker, any wharf guest
who appears out of no place: my squatting turnip
          rump weighed down
          overmuch by my lightsome nylon
     book bag, shoulder

               slung. . . . Airy, nimble,
          buoyant, he is the whole uplift,
          the mass between his clavicles: hidden
mancoil essence wedged
     between shoulder blades
          is poised to spring cloudwise,

skyward, ever,
his walk ascendant in every sandaled—
or barefooted—step; his moves, whether stoops, lateral
        swings, or stretches,
          all are pitch of shoulders on verge,
     verge, verge of flight.

              When he spreads his arms,
        they are wings sucking updraft,
        they are his ship's tiers of sails unfurled
and billowing; *he billows*
    by his breath and the lilt
      of easy glowing talk, and he'll take
        me, or anyone
who consents to be carried, a gladsome
pard, a passenger, into this airborne wide ambrosia
        he contains within
        and diffuses around him, always,
    like a parachute,

            great happy balloon,
      or third lung, expansible,
        which he can inflate outside his body—
with ample room to spare
    for a heady surplus of mates.
      Spare idioms bristle in his cadence.
      His few words—
scraped clean—nourish an ethic of high seas
camaraderie. . . . I've nearly forgotten to scan his face.
      A few quick glances
       give me, by turn and turnabout,
    fine cross between

youthful Lee Marvin
(days of Brando in *The Wild One*)
and Henry Miller lookalikes, as I, now
uprisen from dock stoop,
two heads shorter than he,
idle around his lithe frame, taking in
various profiles,
never two alike. To an obtuse tourist eye,
he's your slovenly lax middleaged hippie with pirate's
wicked leer held back,
this dour mental snapshot sealed
by brightest flash

of his lone earring,
silver-gleamy in mist and haze.
Turns head from side to side, as he chats,
winding the rope coil
at his feet around swelled hive
bulging from his wrist to armpit: seen
from a distance,
it could be mistaken for a triple-width
hemp forearm. Looking closer, steady on, I see telltale
clue that Skyjack's
no common lout: his earring
an inverted fishhook,

its amazing wide eye
pointed earthward, dangling thin
strand of fishline like a needle threaded,
ready to hand for use.
You might suppose a wild cast
by one of his novice fishermates

caught him, thus,
in the ear lobe, which he kept as good luck
token—our hooked escapee a human cousin to Moby Dick
          trailing his multi-
             pronged crown of splintered harpoons,
     flung sea javelins.

Lifestyles Prince

Patrick's mum, a Swiss Countess, mails three thousand gilt postcards
to their whole sprawled family, friends, all friends of friends,
announcing—as one might a royal wedding or jazz festival—
her son's up-and-coming forty-five-second take
on "Lifestyles of the Rich and Famous":
a much-trimmed segment
of his original three-minute interview
debut, taped by *old majestic larynx* himself,
perennial emcee. Card bushels are dispatched, a few hundred
per hour, dark to dawn to dusk—one breathless weekend, by a trio
of couriers (her relay team, running their never-ending cycle of shifts),

posted, scrupulously,
to some four or five continents. She'd
researched, with utmost care, those telecom
satellite networks servicing each remote corner of Planet
pinpointing up-to-the-minute times, dates; trickiest for island
nations and dependencies which might have to rely on thirdhand rerun
serial rights, plus weeks or months of delays down the road,
or sea-lanes, whichever the case: exact starting times
gold-engraved on each of the sidereal galaxy
of cards. . . . Patrick's grand moment,
his coming out, globally,

Mum terms it. Born in a Swiss castle, raised and schooled in London,
Pat threw over a promising legal career as barrister, youngest
Queen's Counselor appointee in years, to join the staff
of posh Malliouhana Hotel, Anguilla's lone swank
World Class Inn; he advanced, swiftly,
to an upper-echelon post:

food-and-beverage manager. *It's a job*
for which I must wear many hats, often 3 or 4
at once, Patrick sighs, as this most recently anointed
Lifestyles Prince tours us through concrete stalls and colossal
archways of the half-finished new hotel wing due to open next season,

palatial rooms half again
wider and higher-ceilinged than suites
of the original bastion, which scored fourth,
just last week, on Lifestyle's short list of ten top
world resorts. Our Patrick, roguish, curlyheaded, whose natural
swagger keeps his husky square-shouldered physique tilted and strutting
just this side of portly—while we fall in with his good-natured
rollicking brisk pace down gravel walkways of worksite,
vacant today, Sunday—chants a paean of praise
for the vast island labor force set
to resume work tomorrow.

Patrick mutters a curse, under his breath, at that TV scriptwriter
who shrank his eloquence to so few seconds of world satellite
air time. What is his main job detail? I ask. Forget
the official worksheet mandate, says he. Hell,
it's those afterhours off-duty foulups
that keep me screwloose
and dizzy. Last Friday, f'rinstance.
A little past twilight, vespers and evensong
churchbells just rung off, I'm gamely making it
with a bonny divorcee who'd obtruded, rap-rap-rap, at my door
beside the SERVICE ELEVATOR (indeed, that plaque could be my title:

I'm summoned to uplift,
or *elevate*, no few frisky lonelyhearts),
her pretext to scare up some ice; or hairnets,
was it? curlers, tampons, whathaveyou—soon my bedside
Mayday phone starts a fearsome clatter just prior to Nirvana
of giddy blinding sweets, all truth serums aspurt. I swear the wicked
roar of the telephone tore the receiver from its black hook
since I cannot recall lifting mouthpiece from cradle.
The newlywed bridegroom in a posh bridal suite
below my spare blank efficiency groans
he needs me "posthaste"

to "look into" (Lord, I beg you, those exact words) his "ladylove's
sudden bellyache." I spring wildly from my dustbin quarters
of a room, half-in/half-out of my bell-bottom pants
damn near spraining my ankle when he grapples
my shoulder bones swung toward him
around the stairwell
descent; and in less than a minute,
we three go bumping down backalley jerkwater
road to the one Cottage Hospital on Crocus Bay Hill
(high point of the island, the high-low summit, we dub it),
our mad threesome now squeezed in frontseat of this topless, sideless

four-wheel-drive moke,
she howling like a mare about to foal.
He keeps her head jammed, vicelike, in his lap
until his knee starts hammering the bloody stick shift
from my clasp, her legs dangled over the low-cut half door,
when three young Sandy Bay lads come hurtling before my windshield

making me brakestop on a dime, my two loose seatmates thrown
headlong into the dash, neatly bounced back to exact
front seat posture, as if performing odd stunts
on a lateral trampoline. I holler, wave
at those reckless lads

to make way and stand clear, while two blokes are lifting a third—
doubledup in pain—over my back seat; one halts my rear wheels
with his legs, shouting: "Dis boy's a goner, him bleed
to daith, carry he to de hospital right quick,"
his blood-spattered face so distorted
I hardly recognize Rudy,
our star junior cook, whose lower lip,
inflated like a balloon, puffs up all the more,
even as I glare at moonlit face toppling into rumble seat.
But Axel's voice rings clear, he another of our kitchen staff
loyalists, and I look back at Rudy, who sports a glittery ornament

embedded in his lip's
blue crack: *a bent fishhook,* his flesh
so swelled around the curled tip, I must squint
to make out thin shaft—trailing those snarls of gold
fishline. . . . So we burn rubber, hotfooting it to this isle's
sole Emergency Wing with two near casualties in tow: gourmet whiz
Rudy bellowing, nonstop, all but squelching her ladyship's
muffled sobs and whimpers. . . . Young doctor on the ward,
he too stretched six ways at once, interrupts
the near-completed delivery of a baby
to snip the hook wire

from Rudy's great bulbous lip, slaps an ice pack on his face, glances
at Missus: *Must operate,* says he, *O never in a million years
on this island,* says Hubbie. *Operate now, or she croaks.
Peritonitis doesn't sit on its hands and wait—
it spreads like brushfire.* Doc whirls
him through the ward's
revolving doors, opens her just in time
to stop the poison, crazed Hub returns, stares
past Doc's shoulder in mid-cutting, and faints at sight
of infection burgeoning everyplace he looks in exposed belly
cavities—while cooing husband on next bed cradles his justborn son.

I.V. Runaway

1.

Sundown. The windup
of my first day's slithering drives,
from one end of Anguilla's twinbeached wriggly-eel
sweep to the other,
both seas visibly ablaze at once
from any land vantage
of the road's sixteen-mile strip (most hills
so shallow, even that indolent one speed pedal biker's
oblivious to dips and rises), we ascend
this low coral isle's
highest bluff, and park at the overlook ledge.
Crocus Hill, two-hundred-sixteen feet
above Crocus Bay,

seems a Carib
Himalaya, though no ears pop for heights
as they do for scuba reef deeps . . . Ten steps back
from mock cliff, we glide
into the Cottage West Hospital wing
that squeezes intensive care
and emergency units into a far corner
cubicle of the neon-glary populous maternity ward—
you leap sideways into my shoulder,
dodging a palmgripped
I.V. bottle swung overhead, trailing a tube
loosely adangle: a forearm which steers
the ambulatory I.V.

blocks our passage
through the ward door, refusing to make way
for us. Hah! It's no bumpkin of a novice orderly

muddling out the exit
in our startled faces, as I'd guessed,
the yokel leading a wheelchaired
and beltstrapped invalid hooked to serum
bottle: rather, we've met the convalescent herself—
your afflicted pal Jeanne, none other—I read
in your bemused smirk
and snorts of greeting, who wields I.V. flask
with her own upthrust arm (still affixed,
dribbling punctual glops)

like nightwatchman
briskly hefting his lantern aglow;
thin tube losing itself in the flouncy ruffles
of her white negligee,
installed, stubbornly yet, but where?—
in a nondetected site
of lower abdomen, or beyond . . . Jeanne's
been holding court, we see, with eight or nine chums,
cronies in the far-flung social set
of expat photo
journalists, travel writers, et cetera, that mixed
bag of transients and native islanders.
With her free hand

she waves signals
(choir leader and concertmasterly moves),
directing twin streams of the visitor traffic
flocked around her—indoors
and outdoors, by turns—across the portal,
a nonstop overflow
exodus from the crammed boxy hospital room.
All the while, one matronly silverhaired nurse's aid

keeps trying to wrestle the I.V. bottle
        from her fluttery
                grasp, a brief juggling act between our duo
        in the overhead ward stratosphere,
                the frail vessel

                changing hands no less
        than seven times, catch as catch can,
                airborne twice before the sickening clatter
                of smashed glass shards—
        mad gush of bilious sticky coagulates
streaming over our footpath.
                Thereinafter, we each pick our steps
                with care, chary to avoid the tarlike ground patches
gelled to the viscosity of fast-dried
        glue, with our sneakers'
                soles . . . Granny nursemate desists, at last,
        from her futile cat-and-mouse gambits
                to wheedle Jeanne

                back to her ward cot
        for I.V. refittings, when a tallish gangly
                white-bewhiskered ink-black gent intercepts them
                in mid fracas tug-of-war
        over the doorsill scrimmage line, hotly grips
the frantic attendant
                by the underarm: *all knuckly fists & scowls;*
                bleats few words; bristles those white-tipped eyebrows;
darts sprout menace in his forehead's twist
        and tilt! He consigns her
                to Siberia of reception desk, she admonished
        not to desert this clerkly post til day's
                end, on pain of . . .

2.

That knobby bulk
of antique stethoscope, which weighs,
visibly, upon his neck (an old moose's crumply
fallen antlers, a lesser
demon's limp and bedraggled horns), giveaway
he's presiding chief
M.D. of Cottage West Hospital—we're braced
for a wrathful chiding, much provoked by wild filly
of renegade patient, his first, ever,
intensive care escapee
and I.V. runaway . . . But our Jeanne comes off,
in his standup sermonette, as White Duchess
of guests, he Concierge

of a Great Inn,
effusive and fawning in his thanks
for her patronage, she a celebrity and model
visitor to this isle's
most popular villa and social club
entwined—Cottage West!
Quick intros, we to "Royal Crown Colony's
Head Doctor": Jeanne plies unction of civil graces,
her move to tie his hands—not to say tongue—
with clever slipknots
of social amenity, and dismiss him, thus,
with courtly wave of her wrist, or snap
of fingers. But if she's

more adept prattler,
he, suaver yet, outfinesses her—who,
spun about, gently but firmly, like a partner

in tango, lets herself
be swept behind doorjamb: poor woman
taken aside for a verdict,
upshot of his scrupulous cool diagnosis.
We overhear tag ends of hushed phrases. *No life threat.*
False appendicitis. Just a case of swelled
vessels, inflammation
in your plumbing, he says, winking coyly.
Whazzat? She flushes. *Run that past me*
once more. He matches

her shrill rising voice
with his broadest grin: *INFLAMED FALLOPIAN*
TUBES! Take a holiday from bed sports. She wheezes
a vapid apology,
glum promise of sorts, and darts away
from his long-fingered pinch
of her collar, then draws us after her
withindoors to a low bed at dead center of the mobbed
maternity ward, which might pass for an over-
booked house party.
We three squeeze together, seated on one edge
of Jeanne's bed, while other family
overspills clutter

three sides, hardly space
enough left in mid mattress for her to recline,
with or without her I.V. bottle (long since smashed
and forgotten). Half-dazed,
still, by the doctor's blunt ultimatum
for her near-term amours,
Jeanne's distracted—but gives us the lowdown
on her quixotic past forty hours. She can't have slept

"3 winks," what with constant "relay teams of guests,"
　　many total strangers
　　　　asking intimate questions about "my progress,"
　　all too familiar with the hush-hush
　　　　details of her malady.

3.

Ah yes, heard
　　all about you, don't you know,
　　　　the last dreary symptom down to the ground:
　　or words to that effect,
yet I've never met these folks before.
　　Everybody else's dirty linen vilely washed
　　　　right under my turned-away
　　　　　　nose! Nights, here,
　　　　　　　　are pandemonium itself, no letup
　　　　　　　　　　to inane crises.
　　　　　　　　　　All female inmates of any age, from eight
　　　　　　　　to eighty, are stowed away in *the zoo:*
　　　　　　　　this free-for-all

maternity
　　bedlam, a barnyard hodgepodge
　　　　lumping all gals into that one ashcan
　　of mamahood and ageless sex . . .
Last night, four women, in quick conveyor
　　belt turnover, were frisked and scuttled posthaste
　　　　from the oblong delivery table
　　　　　　behind pasteboard
　　　　　　　　partition—at the ward's far end—
　　　　　　　　　　to their recovery beds.

The tots, still half-sticky with birth plasmas
(amniotic fluid, blood, and whatnot),
were nestled, already,

in dope-sleep
mom's armpit, or clamped, toothless
gum-gnawing, at one breast. A quartersize
primo runt, blotchy tricolored
ripe for an incubator, rasped for breath
beside a whimpering teenage unwed mother of three.
Fathers, never sent home, are rushed
to gagaeyed wife's
bedside, like as not carrying newborn
babe laid out flat
on two open palms like a loaf of just-sliced
bread on a platter, or fresh bouquet
of flowers waved

under damsel's
nose for a sample sniff, or taste,
as if she could object to this tart flavor,
that fragrance, and send
the offspring back to the oven for more spice,
caraway seed, a tad more browning for that crust.
Those fathers, I say, have no sense
of timing: slaphappy,
verging on blackout from sleep-lack,
they go stumbling
about the ward dark, trip over wrong beds
(scared sleepers emit wails of outrage),
bump one another, lose

their bearings
　　　on the ward's bed-jumbled layout.
　　　　　In the wee hours, today, one stocky man fell
　　　foremost upon me, sighing
and chanting his wife's name, over and over,
　　　　though I'm sure it was all a ruse to jump my bones,
　　　　　　and no accident. But mostly,
　　　　　　　it's your normal
　　　　　　　　well-meaning blokes who get lost
　　　　　　　　　and crawl haywire
　　　　　　　　　zigzagging the ward. Then, too, a few bozos
　　　　　　　get so hot to trot with the missus,
　　　　they start to groove—

no mere foreplay,
　　　I tell you—on the next child-to-be.
　　　　　Now all's a pawing and pigrooting to drown
　　　those feeble wifely protests,
squelched, at last, in her breathless gasps
　　　and puffs. . . . Many husbands, a few toddlers as well,
　　　　　are given to endless meanderings
　　　　　　from wall to wall,
　　　　　　　corner to corner, in the wavery
　　　　　　　　bed floor maze: dark
　　　　　　　to dawn. Though it may be, now and again,
　　　　　a ten- or twenty-minute late respite
　　　from hobblings and gropings

of displaced kinfolks
　　　brings me to the edge of twilight
　　　　　sleep, light doze, catnap, when I'm stunned
　　　awake: volleys of prayerful
mumblings and incantations! A few oldest

women, side by side, shuffled between new mothers
and the ten-year-old tonsillectomy,
count their rosary
beads, and keep vowing a future
of all good deeds—
one by one by one, in each counted breath:
a chorus, two or three chanting at once . . .
So it is they plead

with a deity
for their recovery from illness:
Please, Lord, beat out de devil from me laig
gout; or else, *Keep me alive*
just one more week, one day, six hours.
Click, click, click of the bead prayers, breath counts,
once more, again, and it's daybreak!
By breakfast, scandal
mill's back in full swing: a few newsmen,
toting big cameras
on shoulder or hip, pick their way—crafty and sly—
between the beds, chasing down tips on ribald
stories of our day.

 IV

The St. Kitts
Monkey Feuds

The St. Kitts Monkey Feuds

1.

Denholm, the Brimstone Hill society's current
Vice President,
    who migrated from Mauritius to St. Kitts
        six years back,
    was ambushed by several clumped troops of Vervets—
wave after wave
    of *the varmints*—while jeeping uphill to work
        this morning,
    earlier than usual, catching the first light
at six: monkeys
    so thick on one stretch of road he couldn't see
        dirt passage
    ahead, no view beyond them, no view between

the dense clans,
    no way to count the hundreds—*the most I'd ever*
        laid eyes on . . .
    Denholm vowed never again to drive up here, alone,
at this hour,
    hardly knows what gave him such a fright: to date,
        no reports

    of monkey horde attacks on cars, or humans on foot,
but he rolled up
    his windows, fastened and battened down all canvas
        flaps of his jeep
    roof canopy, and cowered in his seat bucket, while
the chimp swarm
    slowly thinned out; a few juveniles sliding paws

over windshield,
   tongues lapping side mirror, teeth nipping aerial,
door handles.
   No shyness any more, they grow bolder and bolder—
      recalcitrant—
   from twilight to dawn, then beat a wistful retreat

at full daybreak.
   Curious and balmy, playful they are, he surmises.
      No harm in it.
   But he shivers to think of their numbers, and oh,
how swiftly
   they multiply unchecked, no Natural Enemies to keep
      their overspill

   in balance—as in their African homeland. "Our Vervets'
Happy Hour," says
   Denholm, "commences at dusk, just a few darkling shades
      past twilight.
   You may chance upon troops of thirty or forty, who
will freeze up
   at your approach, but they hold their ground: intrepid,
      not chary shy
   as even months ago. They hang together. And if you
walk up to them,
   they seem to flaunt the new boldness in your teeth,
      won't even flinch
   at hand's touch, but I shan't recommend you put them

to that test.
   It seems they know they outnumber us by a wide
      margin already,

and they may know that both Time and Numbers favor
their survival
    preponderance over ours—so I fancy: their tameness
      is never easy

    or just playful, but quietly embattled. A far cry
from domestic
    pets or zoo animals! That steely grim reaper's stare,
      eyes riveted
    to some tree or view in the distance, always sweeps
past your face . . .
    O how they must know our Tribe's been gunning them
      down, failed try
    to decimate their population—they shall not quail
nor forgive,
    believe it! And do not make household pets of any
      but the most wee
    newborns: once they come into their own full command,

autonomy
    in the wilds, it's too late to force a swing back
      to familial
    bent toward humans—least to be trusted as playmates
for toddlers
    or infants, as all too often they are espoused,
      adopted. . . ."

2.

No word of the monkeys in guidebooks or tourist
brochures: natives seem to ignore them, why? I sense
a conspiracy of denials, or quiet dread,

lurking behind all monkey jokes tossed off, absently,
in the marketplace—town center or boondocks. . . .
Wild monkeys, so plentiful and easily trapped

with rudimentary snares, make the ideal subjects
for lab study. I devote a half day to tracking down
Vervet research camps, based in secluded forest

remote from the public eye—perhaps to elude
tourists & locals, alike. Three monkey task forces,
led by doctors and scientists, flourish in St. Kitts's

outback. The most recent encampment, of four years
duration, follows the tutelage of renowned
United States neuro-surgeon, who, seeking clues

to a cure for Parkinson's disease, concocts savage
experiments with caged Vervets (animal rights' folks,
without fail, stage their yearly mild protests):

drugs, electric probes & tissue carvings. . . . Miles
inland and uphill, the Primatologists' camp
holds longest tenure—3 to 4 decades entrenched—

hellbent, till the 21st Century, or longer,
to prove SPECIATION has turned its magic corner
in the St. Kitts wilds: *Evolution's Leapfrog*

to a total new species of monkey catapulted
before our generation's chosen eyes, sweet gift
for us all to witness (*his* eye on Nobel Prize,

no doubt), the usual snail's pace of progress
from one Animal Gene Pool to the radical next one
down the line *sped up*—such is the lab team's

claim: accelerated, as it were, by wild swings
in climate, flora and fauna, soil composite,
et cetera. The Primatologists' findings,

all based on sizes and shapes of body parts, timings
of process or function, ill served they may be
to measure anything but the small animals' slight

physiques! For such be the middling low regard
in which they're held, in secret, by that colleague
of a third neighbor camp: Montreal psychiatrist,

on extended leave from McGill Medical School's
senior faculty—here to explore the *Social
Dynamic* of monkey clans, free and on the loose

in their natural surround. A twenty-year stakeout,
thus far, since Dr. Elkin first set out to delineate
a true and accurate Vervet *mental health model,*

for he would hope to draw many parallels, or psychic
links, between human and monkey social relations,
whereby to cast fresh light on symptoms of incurable

Depression and Paranoia. . . . Doc Elkin's arrival,
delayed an hour by overlong meanderings in the bush,
I feel the aura of his approach before I hear

wispy voices in the distance, a garrulous prattle
not unlike monkey gibber: phantom   elder   trunk
freckled ash-white   sweeps   dancelike   past fronds

& tall stalks of foliage, long arms looping high
overhead, shoulder moves in sync with his voice pitch,
upper body twists enhancing the rigor of speech.

Vocal lessons, I hear: snatches of pedagogy
extemporized on the run, to guest or young apprentice,
alike. . . . Well fooled was I, by his native staff

& domestics: *he not on island this week*   *him travel*
for days, months   —this spiel a protective sheath
to guard him from snoops, newshounds, jealous rivals,

myself . . . But no specter or mistful ghost: this advance
of a robust, highstepping broad figure   bare-chested
longwhitebearded   silverhaired hanks ringleted

over shoulder   outblazed by tousled-fur   whitetipped
shiny curls, thickish pelt of chest hair   *(new species*
of monkey, indeed) . . . I catch him visibly wince—

by a keen face muscle effort control it, his strong
revulsion contained—to behold me, perched on porch rail,
pencil and notepad at the ready, he much practiced

in dispatching the likes of those who would violate
the quiet nobility of his task. But I see his repugnance
pale and sink, upon clasping my hand-proffered plea.

3.

Only five
minutes, perhaps ten,
        can he spare to hold forth a minilecture
        on his two decades, thus far,
        of monkey research. Mid Seventeenth Century, our

                Vervet story commences.
            French military bosses, who maintained
                the colonial outposts
            in French West
                    Africa, sent all lower-class
                        infantrymen and cadets to Gambia
                        and Senegal ("pits of the Continent"), where worst
                            diseases of that Age were most rampant.

            In soldier families, monkey pets grew
            so trendy, no wife would stroll to local park or market
            without her pet Vervet
                perched on forearm or shoulder, puff ball baby
                curled in straw hat's wide brim, perhaps, as in classic oils
        and charcoal sketches of the period; or coupled
        with human infant

in doll buggy,
two exemplary sets
        of ears bobbing over the side bar: the pink,
        the white-furred, black flat nose
        peeping out. . . . When France lost sea wars to the Brits,

                Senegal and Gambia were
                the first poker chips to be traded at Treaty

Auction; the British Royal Navy
wives and kids,
          allured by the classy French styles,
               inherited those prize house pets, monkeys—
first imported to Barbados & St. Kitts, unnoticed,
               perhaps, since one or two pets per family,

     at most, migrated, and no census records
     were kept, nor quarantine limits set. Monkeys, like pet
cats or parakeets, were ignored
     by perfunctory customs and immigration
     officials of their day. . . . So began the vast monkey clans
of Barbados, St. Kitts and Nevis, what with slightly more
than a thousand chimps

imported
to start with. Barbados
     drew the line first, forbade any new influx
     of monkeys, twenty years hence:
     a total ban, backed by threats of huge fines and jail

          sentences, since Vervets
     had multiplied so fast in Mount Gay province
          where a first soldier encampment
     and military
          colony let a few monkey pets
               escape: then, mating freely in the wilds,
               they proliferated like crazy bacteria. In no time,
               the bite they took out of agriculture

     hit like a plague, blight, or early hurricane
     to ravish burgeoning fruit & veggies crops. By seventeen
hundred, it was too late

to control the population explosion.
    Vervets ingested at least one-fourth of their body weight
per day, menaced all crops: watchdog stakeouts were left
overnight to patrol farms

against hordes
of the marauder monkeys—
    snarly curs tied to long ropes, which kept them
    in range of ripening fruit.
    But monkeys outwitted the wardens, stripped all plants

        nearing harvest, just outside
      the orbit of doggie twines, while staying free
        and clear of the growlers'
    nips, immune
        to barks and howls. And at last,
           the monkey troops planned raids, cunningly
           (if we had printouts or blueprints of their sorties,
           they'd serve us well at pro-football lineups,

    or small-scale military skirmishes):
    while one squad of Vervets taunted a patrol mutt, held him
  at bay by swiping at his ears
    or muzzle with outstretched paws, another flank
    cut behind his tail to zip through a row of Christophene
globes or grapefruits—so quickly were all shrubs
stripped bare, even those nearest

the stake-chained
sentinel. . . . Thus, by turn
    of the Century, all three governments banned
    the monkeys from their shores—
    too late, no way to banish wild platoons of the bush.

Few more than one thousand pets
had slipped into all three isles, while today
we estimate their number
much in excess
of fifty thousand in St. Kitts,
alone, more than the combined human
census of Nevis *and* St. Kitts, as of Nineteen Ninety.
If the monkeys multiply by quantum leaps,

so, today, do the legions of bounty
hunters, hired by police chiefs of St. Kitts and Barbados.
This thriving new career
sector provides fresh employment, steady
and lucrative, for perhaps a third of the idle workforce
who get paid twice—once by the State for each head
of slain prey, yet again

by our food
processing plants, which skin
and butcher the carrion for its pricey meat,
though the hides be worthless.
Of late, local Animal Rights activists are sorely vexed,

their diatribes of outrage
against the monkey massacres fast heating up
in Underground Press, protest rags
forbidden sale
to foreign visitors or tourists.
The Prime Minister, hoping to offset
groundswell of public spleen, floods the town civic
centers, markets, and rural outback

with thousands of colorful broadsheets
and fliers proclaiming a pale justice: since Vervet monkeys
have *pillaged* and *despoiled*
most farmers' prime fruit and veggies crops,
the valuable food source must be replaced by fair quotas
of monkey sirloin, monkey flank steak, not to downplay
fine monkey stews & soups

which become,
today, a gourmet delicacy
in best chefs' recipes—fit to rival green
turtle soups, famed worldwide.
The town councils, in turn, sponsor award competitions,

prizes for new hit songs,
top stories and poems, rhymed and unrhymed,
free verse, bolstering the virtues
of monkey foods,
monkey eaters: vitamins, nutrients,
plus new antibodies building immunity
to a vast catalog of ills and diseases—all credited
to our beneficent monkey-rich diets.

A whole mythology springs up at grassroots
carnivals—new folklores, in form of songs, riddles, proverbs,
and children's bedtime tales
extolling the monkey food panacea. A series
of free pamphlets and chapbooks are printed, touting health
gains from the new Wonder Drugs, antitoxins,
refined in local chem labs

from monkey
glandular secretions, monkey
    blood serums; while monkey-derived powders
    and tablets are offered for sale,
    dirt cheap, in local pharmacies, widely held to curb

            many common or exotic ills,
        alike: doubly ironic, since both Senegalese
            and Gambian Green Vervet monkeys
        are supposed—
            by many medical research teams—
                to be original carriers of the Aids
                Virus! Hushed rumors, these, can hardly dampen bold
                War Cries bellowed at our public rallies

        by paid factotums who kowtow to the Chief—
            threefold slogans, the popular catchwords: *Longevity. Wisdom.*
        Sex Potency, all promised
            to those who consume sufficient minimum
            daily dosage of monkey protein, or monkey serum elixirs,
    which can be imbibed, today, at small cost
    in many popular sodas,

canned *Purée*
of Vervet Gland extracts,
        and food byproducts. Superior athletes, some
        quoted in ads on radio or TV,
        others quoted on labels of bottled monkey oil supplement,

            make repeated claims—new record
            wins in races and soccer matches are best enhanced
                by monkey foods, which surpass, even,

                    the illegal
                        steroids, but without health risks
                            of the latter. All current Star Testimonies
                            agree! Monkey's choice Manna for long-distance runners,
                                swimmers, bikers & muscly body builders. . . .

            4.

Kittitians feed on them. Vervets, ever, the most populous
                    monkeys in disease-
            ridden countries of the African Continent, hardy
                survivors for the many past Millenniums,
            these, *our durable forebears,* be touted by the Islanders
                as Health Food—
            but to justify mass killings and butcheries,
                the forests all one
                    sprawled

slaughterhouse. . . . Hunters disembowel & skin fresh-caught
                bounty on the spot,
            hoping to command higher returns by selling directly
                to the general public—folks met randomly
            at roadside or in the bush. But mad outcries, vile clashes,
                on increase
            of late, keep erupting between monkey headsmen
                and those families most
                    endeared

to their monkey pets, six or seven to a household perhaps,
                monkeys, cats & dogs
            all at play with human kids, indeed the whole nursery
                behaving like offspring of one elder dog

or cat—the children loving them like human siblings.
        Schizoid traumas
now develop, to one degree or another, in most
        family homesteads,
            monkeys

still the most popular domestic pets. How difficult it becomes
        for rugged grownups,
        much less children, to reconcile their monkey brethren
           with widespread monkey carnage and massacre,
        even on principle; but when the voracious bounty hunters
        take sniper
pot shots at family Vervets cavorting with infants
        in houseyards or school
           playgrounds,

the parents—irate vigilantes—vow to avenge the wild shootists'
        transgressions. . . . *Worst case*
    hits cited in the news. Deputized huntsmen, called up
        before government magistrate, must answer
    to grim charges: gundown of baby monkey astroll hand-in-hand
        with child owner;
    tree perch hunter shoots monkey in arm's embrace
        of child, his stray shots
           (*bullets*

misfired, so he pleads) striking dog and pet bunny; last case
        the most scandalous
    on the Civil Court Judge's docket: child herself winged
        twice, one cartridge lodged in left shoulder,
    the other, mere flesh wound, nicked her thigh. . . . No child kills,
        child disablings,
    as yet, but grave incidents of juvenile hits

by *stray crossfire*
    (though most

wounds go unreported for fear of repercussions, hunter reprisals
    against whole families)
    show marked increase, week by week, as government pressure
      to decimate the wild monkey clans, mounts.
    Bounty hunters get away with all-but-murder, so much license
      to kill prey,
    no limits, few penalties they be held subject to.
      The State Coffers
        pay out

highest wage to hunters who gun down a hundredfold per week;
    but for all the thousands
    killed, thousands eaten, thousands butchered & meat canned
      in new local canneries, or bottled monkey
    loins pickled with herbs & spices, fermented oil-based recipes
      run amuck,
    the Vervet multitudes are barely diminished. Today,
      green monkey throngs,
        more fecund

than ever, seem to burgeon everyplace in the bush, much nearer
    the village environs,
    and rash monkey shootings threaten to jinx the tourism
      industry. Areas near town centers frequented
    by tourists, high-risk zones, are declared strictly off limits
      to roving hunters:
    if they be witnessed picking off monkeys by upper-
      echelon dignitaries
        from France,

Britain, Canada, or the United States, they must face penalties
          much severer than those
     prompted by sniper fire killings of family pets. Vacation-
          giddy tourists' public-vented outrage, even,
     may cost sharpshooter huntsmen their lawful bounty license. . . .
          In Barbados,
     St. Kitts and Nevis, perhaps by joint edict of councils
          in all three nations,
               restricted

areas are zoned and beflagged out-of-bounds to Vervet hunters,
          on pain of large fines
     and prolonged license revokings. Yet most monkey-populous
          sectors, such as the original Mount Gay region
     of first wild monkey colonies in Barbados, are ariot with rival
          bounty-hunter
     factions, each positing their exclusive territorial
          boundaries: who defy
               other gangs

to cross strict borders & risk machete-hacked limbs, like Big City
          Western drug cartels
     and gangland mobsters slicing up the pie of prime city buyers,
          guarding each wedge of piecrust with their lives
     on the line. . . . But all hunter carnage has barely put a dent
          in three isle
     monkey populations, still far surpassing the human
          numbers, hands down, due
               to absence

of Natural Foes, replete in the African outback where green Vervet
          hordes are held in check
     by some five species of predatory cats, in all sizes, which

can outrun them on the ground, out-trapeze them
in the treetops—acrobatics the realm of quick survival jousts,
        not riflery
and gun marksmanship. Ourselves the only slayers here,
        we men poorish stand-ins
            for leopard,

tiger, margay, jaguar and puma. . . . Meanwhile, city folks applaud
        those armies of bounty
hunters taking up the slack of unemployment, which provides
        a revenue boost for social services, plus money
to salve hurts of the economy. But the bush-war crisis worsens
        in country home-
steads, where three or more generations of Vervets
        have flourished as full-fledged
            child partners.

   5.

Dr. Elkin builds his research quarter to open into the wilds—
            his vantage a doorway or window
        to the monkey's natural habitat:
        no cages, no zoos,
        no confining the specimen of study
to a quarantined lab.
In his own glide of person, blent into backdrop, he's hiddenly
            visible—as hunters be shrouded
        from bird view on lake face,
        ensconced in duck
    blind: who has devised a unique walk,
half hip-rotation,
half back-and-shoulder whirl, more akin to monkey's locomotion
            than any human's I've yet beheld;

while his lungs, drawing breath
a softer way, keep
the monkey clans tame and fearless
of his free-swishing
advance. Himself a mobile Eye, passive uninterfering witness,
he takes in the shuffle, reshuffle
of all norms in the Vervets'
social milieu.
Most wayfaring monkeys, at large, prowl
freely in the bush
when no scavenging bounty hunter looms near. They meander
in flocks. Troop size ranges
from eight to forty—perhaps
twenty, on average.
The larger units, more sedate, installed
in partial homestead,
cohere around an eldest female—the Head Matriarch revered
as a command ambience, or Guru.
Nearing peak size, a dominant
young male lures
frisky handful away, forming splinter herd
of eight to twelve,
who, in turn, pick up solitaries, gathering forces to become
a full-fledged troop of twenty.
But in times of clan turmoil,
they reconnoiter—
timid and sheepish—back to their home base,
to beg sage counsel
in form of calming nods, gasps, sighs by the reigning Queen.
And she does quell the hysteria,
restoring balance with her soft
tempos, deep reserves
(such power aquiver, you'd suppose she wore

crown, waved a wand:
literal scepter might be the stripped shiny branch she flicks—
                    you must see this queer masquerade
                    to believe it), while she squats
                    in tree-fork throne. . . .
            Soon the renegade herd splits anew, perhaps
adding new members
to its ranks. A normal midsize troop—which fast proliferates
                    into a moderately stable unit
            some six weeks to two months
            after first rebels
        break from the pack—comprises near equal
numbers of males
and females; but no fewer than two-thirds shall be juveniles,
                    which gives a reliable quotient
            of how swiftly Vervets breed,
            no keeping down
        their sex play or frenetic propagation . . .
"Wait long enough,
stay quiet," says Elkin. "You may catch them in mating frenzy.
                    It breaks out like your soccer
            match at the half-time bell.
            So sudden it is,
        no early warning signals we can pick up
(my personal radar,
at least, not sensitive enough): wideopen orgy! Mostly hetero.
                    Youngest mate with oldest. All
            combos Gung Ho. Hots keynote—
            frequent switcheroos,
        rotation of partners so swift & constant
we cannot track
the turnabouts: sex relay teams! Juggling acts, whereby sleight
                    of hand befuddles your eyes'

tardiness. Vervets perennial
random maters:
in humans, we'd call it promiscuity carried
to the Nth Power.
Indeed, as we watch the verve & gusto of mating circus heat up,
mate switches seem to explode,
incrementally, on the upside:
Quantum Leap
sex bouts, I'd term it. Gibbons, you may know,
the only Primates
proved, to this day, to be truly monogamous: but Vervet monkeys,
though not known pair bonders,
form tightly-knit ties, always,
within their troops.
Once the Clan unit is fixed, they remain
loyal to the clique
for long durations. Though splinter groups are led by dominant
youngish males, the larger droves
drift back to matriarchy,
once a revered
elder female emerges—groomed to be Empress.
Whenever herd size
grows to twenty-five or thirty, the queen hunt process unfolds.
Three or more candidate rivals
may primp & dazzle, but Vervet
Grande Dame
comes into her own, and her firm hegemony's
never in doubt.
She reigns for *Life Term.* Wrongly, we presume our family ties,
social mores, are more civilized
than norms of the *lower* Primates.
Given the lie,

in St. Kitts. Take nursing Vervet's instinct
toward mutants,
mental retards or deformed offspring—she adamantly refuses
                    to feed or care for that deviate
              babe. Her troop says a flat Nay
              to aberrants,
       won't tolerate dull-minded newborns—starved
and left to die;
monkeys one-up on humans, since they improve genetics of Race
                    by weeding out feebler strains.
              If borderline case be in doubt,
              the troop consults
       our Grande Dame: she, tie-breaker to the last,
ends the deadlock."

6.

Dawn after dawn, Elkin scrutinizes
       the Vervets'
                    communal life in the wilds. He discerns,
                    in time, the clear-cut checks
              & balances at work in the troop: slowly, he feels
       his way toward their full range of mood swings—

                           he can target
              early signals of upcoming storm turbulence,
or pick up happy gush
       of affect, those electric surge highs
              when good feeling spreads to all corners at once
       like sun breaking through cloud.
He comes to sense the next shift, moments before,
              and finds he can predict all near-term social weather

changes, much as uppers or downers
    in those human
        families he monitors in group therapy sessions
        back home in Montreal.
        Rather, his powers to intuit the monkeys' psychic
    climate improves, with the passing months,

        since the remove
    of a few species jumps, the smidgins of genetic
distance between Vervet
    clans and himself, gives him a clarity
      and balance wanting in his intimate closeups
    with humans he so often failed
to help, much less cure, in family counseling.
    The Vervets, in most fleshly and metabolic leanings,

    mirror us: our exact matchups, even,
      for high blood
        pressure and alcoholism; in both cases,
        their population averages
        a mere 5%—like ourselves—the ratio per hundred
    who are most vulnerable to addiction

        or illness: hence,
    the great value of Elkin's research to depict
a near accurate monkey
    health model. His work in the St. Kitts
      bush commenced on pretext of drawing parallels
    to humans; but, of late,
his research leanings have tugged him away
    from the human psyche to pure inquiry of Vervets'

social habits. Yes, their society's
     mind order
          is subtle and complex, which eludes,
               utterly, his colleagues
               in the neighbor site, *hung up on speciation theory,*
     who measure skull sizes, tweak muscles, &c.,

               ad nauseum. . . .
          Thus, Elkin would hope to dispel much falsity
in monkey folklore, lies
     borne of local politics to support
          the war on Vervets, those limitless slaughters;
     still worse, the lies fostered
by *fool species-change claptrap.* For five years,
          he's been putting to his own private test the suspect

case for NEW SPECIES OF MONKEY EVOLVED
     IN ST. KITTS,
               soon to be documented in publications
                    penned by *local hooligan*
                    primatologists. . . . Months back, their camp imported
     unspecified quantities of rare African

               monkeys, strains
          believed to be direct ancestors to our Vervets,
whereby to shore up their weak
     findings. They set about to collect
          raw data of process and function, as measured
     by clumsy body gauges, tests
geared, strictly, to one monkey at a time, one
          by one by one, battered by machines, electric shocks,

drug injections: the poor lab animals
        pushed to extremes
                of hunger & thirst; their muscles, tendons
                    stretched to all limits,
                and beyond, for speed and endurance. But never, alas,
are two or more creatures viewed in a free

                non-lab setting,
            or natural habitat. Now Elkin hires out a dozen-odd
Vervets from diverse imported
    strains, tagged for his private study,
        while the bulk of his fellow researchers travel
    abroad, one noted scientist
leasing subjects from others *in absentia*—who
            treat the small animal stockpile like a lending library.

    First, he commingles six African chimps,
        a mixed blend
                of several imported strains, in enclosed
                    outdoor space: a wiremesh cage
                    encircling trees and shrubs in the wild, to simulate
    a natural locale, as in best modern zoos.

                And he repeats
            this trial and error Vervet population mix-up
with several different troops
    of both imported and native monkeys,
            always in equal numbers—a twinning of foreign
    and local teams, so to speak;
the results are always the same, like magic.
            Local Vervets, strongly dominant, come out the winners

in group free-for-all, get the largest
        share of food
                & drink; champions, too, in rare slugfest
                    mostly settled on squeals
                and bravado of arm wavings, body slaps performed
on themselves, as though to mimic human

                    wrestlers' chest-
            poundings to scare off all wouldbe opponents.
Kittitian Vervets, then,
        seem to vanquish their Senegalese
            adversaries in all contests of aggression.
        Next, if the balanced mix
is left *in situ* for still longer durations,
        a curious pattern of mating habits unfolds, slowly,

but decisively. Two or three discrete
        African strains,
                who resist all impulse to interbreed,
                    soon begin to copulate
                with Kittitian monkeys: transcontinental mating
flourishes unchecked. Again and again,

                most Overseas
            monkeys prefer the Island cousins as mates,
repulse their home buddies. . . .
        Ever a shrewd observer of monkey
            semiotics, Elkin studies the pattern of cues,
        grunts, whinnies, snickers,
as well as hip swings, shoulder lifts, arm twists—
        all forms of body language he's learned to decode

from years of close scrutiny in the bush,
    Elkin's skills
        akin to deciphering a foreign spy system's
          code, flag-wave semaphores,
        or suchlike. All local chimps and imports, he notes,
    fail in joint efforts to communicate

          with each other;
        most cues and signals fly past, sadly go over
the alien sex partners'
    heads. The pain and frustration of lost
      signals, misfires, is obvious in puzzled faces,
    head shakes of quizzical
wonder—yet the mating allure grows strong, ever
      stronger: the crux of Elkin's case against speciation!

    7.

Of late, Elkin's appalled by a shift to great numbers
of underpaid
    mercenaries, joining the St. Kitts monkey war posse
      and bandwagon
    (hundreds of unlawful immigrants, no doubt, imported
for dirt low
    Black Market wage by the government)—to save revenue.
      If divulged
    by the Press, or leaked out to the Populace, the shock
may undermine
    the Town Council's chief rationale for the dramatic
      speedup in pace
    of monkey slaughters: well-paid job detail for hundreds

of unemployed
  native workforce veterans, not to say poor retirees
    living from hand
to mouth, after a lifetime of able-bodied service.
Perhaps dozens
  of these, it seems, shall now be bypassed, to favor
    those dirt-wage

  hirelings, escaped criminal types, homeless wayfarers
from isle to isle,
  no job too tawdry, no pay scale too scant. . . . Inured rage
    of local farmers,
  exacerbated by the marauding monkey hordes' fierce
devastation
  of prime fruit farms grown worse this year, tends to fuel
    the Ruling Party's
  political mandate and clout in escalation of the War
on Vervets,
  more tax revenues earmarked for the battle, looser
    hiring policies
  indulged. . . . Granted, the monkeys—epidemic or menace—

must be stopped
  from devouring St. Kitts's farm crops! All the same,
    I ask, pleading,
  if the Doctor and his scientist cronies encamped
in far outlands
  can persuade the Prime Minister to try to find a way
    to save the Vervets

from brutal massacre. Well yes, he and his close peers
have kept lobbying
    to persuade the VIPs to pay bounty hunters, instead,
        to take monkeys
    alive—catch them in nets and snares, employing modern
tactics developed
    by World Zoo Commissions: baits in pits, or luring them
        with fragrance,
    scents they can't resist, doping them for easy capture,
then stockpiling
    thousands of monkeys in kennels, wide tall cages, stored
        for worldwide
    sale to zoos and research laboratories. Elkin claims

there's enormous
    demand abroad for Kittitian Vervets, in particular;
        their Overseas
    purchase, if promoted as revenue-strong local industry,
would rejuvenate
    the island's shaky economy far better than selling
        dead monkey meat

    for food. . . . But his proposals, struck down by the lower
courts on vague
    technicalities, never reach balloting for free vote
        referendums.
The cartel smuggling mercenaries into St. Kitts, much
the stronger lobby,
    cannot be stopped. And too many vengeful citizens, needing
        a Blood Sport
    Cathartic, crave the ongoing hunt and kill to punish
the perennial crop

destroyers. Elkin continues to tout the great demand
        for live Vervets
in foreign markets—for guaranteed lucrative returns:

a Big Business
        could be nurtured, which might quickly rival Batik works,
                historic books,
        sugar, and shrimp, as St. Kitts's leading export. But the air
is thick with Feud
        Musk, the scent of carnage, revenge, a momentum tough
                to turn around.

        8.

        This year alone,
        the vanguard of government-paid full-time
bounty hunters has tripled—
        only two or three prime zones of tourist capers
                are off limits to the Death Squads. Huntsmen now work
                        in small battalions
                                back in the bush, since monkeys are ambushed,
        often, in droves of forty, and hunters want to make a clean sweep
                of lucky run-ins,

        who seal off the pack
        by encircling Vervets' hideaway or bivouac,
thereby to lose no stragglers . . .
        A common horror—I'm told by youth Animal Rights'
                chaps—is to spot a dozen Hit Men bursting from forest
                        thickets at daybreak
                                lugging on backs, shoulders, heavy baskets
        or net bags, so brimful of monkey carrion that overspill surplus
                of stuffed-doll shapes

leaves a grisly trail
      of corpses in its hurried wake. If, absently,
you ignore their beeline route
      from mid-forest outward to valley clearing,
         you could mistake the pack for fishermen bowed down
            by a record haul:
                  bushelfuls of amberjack or yellowtail, say,
      whole schools of gamefish netted & yanked from the sea in awesome
                  swift ten-minute plunder

      of the pre-dawn Bays,
         as often happens at peaks of fishing season.
But these crews ne'er display
      the eye sparkle and bronze-cheeked allure, necks
         upreared like prancing stallions of the happy fisher
            fleet; proud heroes
                  flaunting their great catch to dawn choir
      of cheerers, the first arrival of housewives, on foot, by donkey,
            wagon, or motorcar,

      to claim fresh flappers—
         most of the batch whipping about in barrels
or nets, as if fighting off
      a tad of unexpected turbulence and rough currents
         at sea, then to burrow back from bay whirlpools to open
            waterway. But no!
                  This quarry of bulk carcass is *stock still*,
      the haulers puffing, faces averted from passersby, eyes downcast,
            no social pride aglow

in this workmanship,
no matter how deft or expert has been the kill. . . .
After two decades encamped here,
Doc Elkin knows every local face. So hunter lads
hide their visage from his glares, whenever he crosses
their paths, by chance,
on his morning stroll: blood of massacre
yet steamy in the air, bloodstains mixed in sweat of their brows,
adrip from leaky baskets.

LAURENCE LIEBERMAN has published nine books of poetry. His work has been widely anthologized; his poems and critical essays have appeared in most of the country's leading magazines, among them *The New Yorker, American Poetry Review, The Hudson Review,* and *Sewanee Review.* The title poem to this collection appeared in *Best American Poetry 1991.* He has received grants from the National Endowment for the Arts and fellowships from Yaddo and the Huntington Hartford Foundation. Lieberman taught English and did research for many years in the Virgin Islands and across the Caribbean and is currently professor of English at the University of Illinois, Champaign-Urbana.